Johann Konrad Wilhelm Löhe

Portrait of a Confessional Lutheran

by

Rev. D. Richard Stuckwisch, M.Div., S.T.M., Ph.D.

Repristination Press
Malone, Texas

© 1994 by the author. Published by permission.

Repristination Press
P.O. Box 173
Bynum, Texas 76631

www.repristinationpress.com

ISBN-13: 978-1461065418

ISBN-10: 1461065410

Table of Contents

Löhe's Early Life and Formative Years 5
Conflicts with the Bavarian State Church 13
Confessional Lutheran Identity 14
Three Books About the Church 20
Motivation for Missions 22
Löhe's Mission and Ministry within his Congregation 24
Löhe's Theology of Liturgical Worship 29
    Liturgy as Prayer 29
    Liturgical Freedom 31
    Liturgical Form 32
    Proper Use of Liturgical Forms and Freedom 43
Löhe's Liturgical Theology in Practice 48
Löhe's Missionary Efforts in America 54
    ... Among German Lutherans 54
    ...Among the Heathen American Indians in Michigan 64
    ...After Missouri: The Founding of the Iowa Synod 70
    The Neuendettelsau Society for Inner Missions 73
Löhe's Local Mission: The Deaconess Motherhouse 74
Löhe's Final Days and Death 77
The Continuing Fruits of Löhe's Efforts 77
Appendix: Löhe's American Contemporaries, Walther & Grabau ... 81
Bibliography 88

4

EPIGRAPH: What is it that I seek? I seek to serve! Whom shall I serve? The Lord through His afflicted and poor one. And what shall be my reward? I serve, anticipating neither pay nor gratitude but out of a sense of gratitude and love; my reward is that I am privileged to serve! And what if in so doing I perish? If I perish, I perish, said Esther, who didn't know Him out of love for whom I would perish and who will not permit me to perish. And what if I grow old in rendering service? Then my heart will rejoice, and the Lord will satisfy me with grace and mercy. I go my way in peace and without anxiety.

LÖHE'S EARLY LIFE AND FORMATIVE YEARS:

Wilhelm Löhe was born into an upper–middle class family of Fuerth, Bavaria, on February 21, 1808. In Fuerth, he lived his boyhood days a few miles from the famous medieval city of Nuremberg—one of the two free cities to sign the *Augustana* in 1530. (cf. Heintzen–1964:14) He had four older sisters (though the oldest one, an epileptic, died when he was nine) and a younger brother, Max.[1] An evangelical merger of Lutheran orthodoxy and Pietism characterized the atmosphere of their family life. Going to church, family devotions and personal piety were stressed. Pietistic tendencies entered especially through parental contact with various "Christian societies," typical of the Awakening in southern Germany. But still, an orthodox Lutheranism that stressed such things as the universal atonement remained the dominant influence. (cf. Heintzen–1964: 14–15)

Wilhelm's father was a successful merchant who also held several honorary civic offices. Though he died in 1816, when Wil-

---

[1] cf. Löhe, *Three Books About the Church*: 2. [Hereafter, cited in–line, according to the format: (3B: 2).]

helm was only eight years old, the elder Löhe had a lasting impact on his son (cf. 3B: 2). He writes: "My father was the foremost person in the world to me, my mother came next, then my sister Anna, the sickly one, yet for whose strength I had great respect." (Schober: 5) Years after his father's death, Wilhelm still remembers one occasion in particular which may well have initiated his life–long love for the Church and Her Ministry: "One time there was a convention of the synod. The pastors of the large diocese of Cadolzburg, to which Fuerth belonged, gathered in the gallery of St. Michael's Church. My father took me, carried me to the highest gallery, lifted me up so that I could look down on the venerable gathering. That view remained with me; I still hold and enjoy it." (Schober: 4)

If Wilhelm's father had an impact on his son while he lived, his death left an even more permanent impression: It was merely the beginning of Wilhelm Löhe's frequent exposure to sickness and death among his loved ones.

> On the day my father died, October 28, 1816—a Monday—I was in school. Our old servant, Susanna, came and got me. As I entered the room, my family was lying on their knees, praying for cessation of the painful struggle... My mother, rising from her prayers, took me by my hand and led me to my father, lying in his death–rattle, put my hand in his and had me, among other things which I don't remember any more, promise that I would never be a disgrace to my precious father in his grave. Barely had I finished my promise when my father stopped breathing, and I was an orphan! (Schober: 5)

Wilhelm's mother, Barbara, who lived to the age of 83, was most instrumental in shaping her son's spiritual development, especially following her husband's death (cf. 3B: 2). She had long considered that he ought to be a minister, but his father had always objected because of the educational expense. As a widow she encouraged her son to pursue the ministry as his life's vocation. Löhe wrote:

> Sometimes my mother would say to my father: "A minister is lost in that boy if you don't let him study." But my dear father did not want to hear of it as the expenses in comparison to

those of the rest of his children seemed out of proportion to him. After my father had died, my mother carried out what she considered to be wise and good. Her love for the office and her church made it desirable for me to choose the ministry for my life calling, despite the fact that she was a widow. I owe her thanks a thousandfold for that. Who knows whether I would have become a Christian if I had not become a pastor! (Schober: 5–6)

Barbara Löhe's personal piety also served as an example to Wilhelm. There were some less than orthodox aspects, as she (like many other Germans of her day) read daily from the *Garden of Paradise* by Arndt (a mystic) and from the *Daily Handbook* by Starck (a Pietist). (cf. 3B: 2) But she also would go to Confession before the Lord's Supper, and this after several days of preparation. Every Sunday, she would read to her children an orthodox Lutheran sermon, usually chosen from Luther's *Hauspostille*. (cf. Heintzen–1964: 15) And she would often pray with Wilhelm. He comments: "It was easy for me to learn what my mother recited to me, and I was happy when she put me to bed at night with: 'I know in whom I believe' or 'Protected with Thy blessing', etc." (Schober: 4)[2]

Already cultivated very early in Wilhelm's spiritual life was a deep love and appreciation for the Lord's Supper, including a vibrant belief in the Real Presence. For instance, many years later as a pastor Löhe describes from memory his regular practice at about the age of twelve:

> In Fuerth every Sunday at 8 A.M. the church bells are rung for Holy Communion. As a rule no one except the communicants was present at the service. But I came and with me an old gray Hospitalist... The old pastor was not a bit more musical than I, but he had a lovely voice, and the way he sang the *Verba testamenti* etc., I have never heard it sung since. The tune he used remained with me and I always sing it from memory when I consecrate through the grace of Jesus. Then when the

---

[2] For a massive collection of prayers, which Löhe himself would years later publish, including Collects appropriate for almost every occasion imaginable, cf. his *Seed–Grains of Prayer*.

old man had consecrated the elements, the choir–master sang the *Sanctus* with power! As soon as he began to sing, my old companion also began to sing along with his screechy voice, and I also sang for all I was worth. In school I never sang for I realized I had no gift for it. But for the service of the Lord's Supper I had a voice and let it come forth. This participation was for me great celebration and joy. (Schober: 7–8)

Löhe's warm embrace of the Sacrament would continue to exert a profound influence on the future pastor throughout his life and in his ministry and liturgical theology. It certainly made his confirmation and first communion a truly blessed event, as he recalls:

I received little instruction in connection with taking part in the Lord's Supper but I preferred to believe that I was tasting blood rather than the lukewarm instructions of my teachers. Yet, what I lacked in understanding the gracious God supplied through His most blessed visitation. I knew in whom I believed and He was close to me during that precious Pentecost hour when I first partook of Holy Communion. This experience of divinely–bestowed bliss has made every returning confirmation period unspeakably rich with the sweet aroma of a holy recollection. (Schober: 8)

Following his confirmation in 1821, Wilhelm left the Latin school in Fuerth to attend the Melanchthon Gymnasium in Nuremberg. (cf. 3B: 3) One of his teachers, Karl Louis Roth, who was also the school's rector, exerted a powerful influence over him. Rector Roth kindled in Wilhelm a "love for the old songs and literature of the fathers." (Heintzen–1964: 17) He exhibited joy in his own religion, and by his "simple preaching of the sweet Gospel" kept the young Löhe "loyal to his Lord and Savior." (3B: 3) For better or for worse, he also involved Wilhelm in the Nuremberg pietistic circles that engaged in devotional meetings and missionary work. (cf. Heintzen–1964: 17)

From the gymnasium, Löhe entered the University of Erlangen in November 1826 and there began his actual theological studies. Here he was influenced by Professor Christian Ludwig Krafft. Professor Krafft was also the pastor of the local Reformed congregation, as well as the chief representative of the *Awakening* in Erlangen. Löhe was not required to attend the lectures of Professor Krafft, but he did so on Roth's recommendation. (cf. 3B: 4) In particular, Krafft's "work on the letter to the Hebrews and pastoral theology... won [Löhe] completely for Christ." (Schober: 10) He deepened both Löhe's respect for the Bible as God's Word and his appreciation of Christ's atonement, to such an extent that Löhe could write: "Although I was reared according to God's Word, and never forsaken by His grace, I owe my spiritual life, humanly speaking, to a Reformed teacher, Professor Krafft of Erlangen. It was he, whom I remember with deep affection, who without knowing it nurtured my love for the Lutheran Church which I carried with me from my youth." (Heintzen–1964: 18)

It is difficult to say just how "Lutheran" Löhe would have remained had he not also spent a semester at the University of Berlin in the spring and summer of 1828. (cf. Heintzen–1964: 20) It was here that he came into contact with Professor Friedrich Strauss, who specialized in Luther and the Lutheran Confessions. (cf. Heintzen–1973: 10) Strauss "pointed out with a holy warmth the majesty of the liturgy, the greatness of sacrificial moments in the service, [and] the labor of the ministerial office," thereby providing a lasting effect on Löhe's future pastoral practice. (Schober: 10) But even more important, he "strengthened Löhe's already awakened ardor for the Confessions and Luther and also helped to negate some of the gross un–Lutheran effects of the pietistic circles." (Heintzen–1964: 20) Henceforth, Wilhelm Löhe would be far more orthodox and confessional than pietistic.

Upon returning from Berlin to Erlangen, Löhe pursued a more focused approach to his studies, which, in turn, sharpened his identity as a Lutheran. He was especially interested in the differences between Reformed and Lutheran doctrine, in particular with regard to the Lord's Supper. And he concluded that the main difference between the two was precisely here: in their disagreement over the Sacrament—which of course was no small matter to Löhe! (cf. 3B: 5) The whole period was a time of critical growth and development for Löhe, as he wrestled and came to grips with the doctrine of the Lutheran Church. As one biographer comments: "Diligent study of the confessional writings, faithful pursuit of Luther's works, penetrating lectures on the Bible increased the knowledge of the young

[Löhe], who did not become a Lutheran due to Pietism, but rather from an acquired Lutheranism into which a sincere and deep, living grasp forced itself, so that to him Christendom henceforth was to be measured only by the two poles—grace and faith!" (Schober: 10) At the same time, Löhe's increasingly confessional orthodoxy was always active in spreading the pure doctrine he was learning. While still a student at the university, he organized a student missionary society and distributed religious tracts—activities of the sort he would support throughout his life. (cf. 3B: 5)

Löhe finally completed his studies at Erlangen and passed his first theological examination in October 1830. (cf. 3B: 6) The examination, held in Ansbach, included a sermon Löhe preached on 1 John 1:8. He was then ordained on July 25, 1831, though he would not receive his first pastorate for another six years (cf. Schober: 10); what followed instead was a long series of "vicarages."

Löhe's first vicarage was with an elderly pastor in his home town of Fuerth. But this arrangement did not work and lasted only a few months because the pastor, who had never before had a vicar, was jealous of Löhe's involvement with the parishioners. (cf. 3B: 7)

The second vicarage assignment was far more successful and pleasant. This time, Löhe was the vicar of Rev. Carl Christian Sommer in Kirchenlamitz. He maintained from the start a good relationship with his bishop and quickly endeared himself to the congregation. Here in Kirchenlamitz Löhe first developed into an outstanding preacher. And in addition to his many regular duties, "at the congregation's request he instituted weekday prayer services and organized Bible study groups, missionary societies, and prayer cells." He was extremely popular with the people, and well–liked by Pastor Sommer. But Löhe managed to attract an enemy in a prominent district judge in Kirchenlamitz. Apparently the judge considered himself especially attacked by Löhe's preaching, although his reasons for feeling this way are not entirely clear. In any case, he brought a variety of false and exaggerated charges against Löhe, and he was finally able to have the vicar removed as of February 1834. (3B: 7–11)

After leaving Kirchenlamitz, Löhe was assigned to be the administrator of the vacant assistant pastorate of St. Giles Church in Nuremberg, a large metropolitan parish. And while at St. Giles, as was becoming standard practice for him, Löhe and his friends organized yet another missionary society. (cf. 3B: 12–13)

In April 1835, after a regular pastor had been called to St. Giles, Löhe became the administrator of the parish in Behringersdorf, a small suburb of Nuremberg. It was here that he passed with the highest possible mark the required second examination for ministerial candidates. And thus he became eligible to hold a full pastoral office in the Church. It was also here in Behringersdorf that Löhe first met a certain girl from Frankfurt on the Main. The girl, Helene Andreae, was temporarily living in Nuremberg and happened to be among a group of Löhe's confirmands. Two years later, she would be his wife. In the meantime, however, Löhe served as the adminstrator of several other congregations, a few months each in the towns of Altdorf, Bertholdsdorf and Merkendorf. Finally, he applied (albeit reluctantly) for a small vacant pastorate in the tiny farming community of Neuendettelsau. He would have much preferred a city church, but his appointment to Neuendettelsau came toward the end of 1836. After a delay of several months (to accommodate his marriage to Helene) Wilhelm Löhe arrived at the small parish on August 1, 1837 and preached his first sermon as pastor the following Sunday. (cf. 3B: 13–14)

It was on July 25, 1837, at the age of 29, that Löhe had travelled to Frankfurt and married the 18–year old Helene (with her parents' permission and blessing). (cf. 3B: 14) But sadly, after only six years of marriage, Helene died on November 24, 1843, leaving Pastor Löhe with four young children to care for and a grief–stricken heart. (cf. 3B: 27) To add to Löhe's grief, less than a year after his wife's death the youngest of his four children also died. The other three children he educated by himself until they were of confirmation age. And except for his mother at times, he had no one to help in caring for their home until his daughter had grown up. (cf. Ottersberg: 172) The impact of Helene's death on the rest of Löhe's life was tremendous, as can be seen, for instance, in his comments on the fourth anniversary of her death: "Whenever I think or talk about it, my greatest joy is still my Helene. I never had any good fortune in life until I found Helene. Since she's gone I die a little bit each day that I live. God be merciful to me and my poor orphans." (3B: 27)

Löhe later remarked that Helene's death had made a "shipwreck" of his personal life, which is no doubt why he never remarried but rather was "wedded to his work on which he lavished tireless devotion." (Heintzen–1964: 23)

The likeness of Löhe's work to a marriage is only heightened by the fact that he spent his entire 35–year ministry as the pastor of Neuendettelsau. During the first ten years, on four separate occasions, he applied for a city pastorate—in Augsburg, Nuremberg, Fuerth and Erlangen, respectively. But after these were all denied, he was apparently content to remain in his little country parish. (cf. 3B: 14) Neuendettelsau was "a quiet German village in Bavaria some twenty miles southwestward from Nuremberg." The parish included one or two neighboring villages, as well, for a total of just over a thousand members (not all that small, really, by modern American standards). "Difficult of access and lonely, it contained an undistinguished rural church [building] and a small parsonage." Pastor Löhe's annual income for the entire 35 years was $250–300. His people were "Franconian peasant stock, rather stolid and set in their ways." (Ottersberg: 170) In retrospect, had Löhe received one of the larger, city parishes, he likely would not have accomplished as much as he did, both in his own congregation and with his worldwide mission efforts. As it was, due to the size of the Neuendettelsau parish and to the length of his tenure, Löhe was able to guide and shape the congregation according to his own high ideals. For Löhe, that meant centering on the Word and Sacraments. (cf. 3B: 14)

To understand properly Löhe's high Word and Sacrament ideals, one must see his ministry in the context of the *Awakening* in 19th–century Germany, for to look at the *Awakening* is to see, on a national scale, a broad reflection of Löhe's personal experience and development. In reaction to the Union Church movement in Germany, along with an ongoing battle against the pervasive Rationalism of the day, forces of Pietism and orthodoxy merged, to some extent, in common cause. But also in the midst of these struggles, Lutheran orthodoxy grew more precise in its own orientation as it sought to return to its roots. In this way, "the orthodoxy of the seventeenth century became the norm for the orthodox evangelical Lutherans of the mid–nineteenth century," including Wilhelm Löhe. Such emphasis on restoration encouraged strong hierarchical tendencies that exalted "the ministerial office and stimulated the desire for the episcopate" as keepers of confessional orthodoxy. These so–called "high church" tendencies also included a revived interest in "the old liturgical traditions and forms," and Löhe in particular "strove to recover more churchly ways" in his own parish and ministry. On the other hand, arising from the more pietistic elements of the *Awakening* were the "vigorous lay philanthropic and evangelistic endeavors known collectively as 'inner mission'." Löhe was undoubtedly influenced by these emphases as well. But whereas most worked across denominational lines in such activities, Löhe worked to establish a distinctively *Lutheran* "inner mission" effort. (cf. Heintzen–1964: 3–9)

Conflicts with the Bavarian State Church:

Pastor Löhe's relationship to the *Awakening* was by no means a merely passive one. In 1848—a year in which everyone was striving for freedoms of all kinds—Löhe took the lead in calling for a separation of Lutherans and Reformed in Bavaria, "on the basis of loyalty to Scriptures, whole–hearted subscription to the Lutheran Confessions, and strict Church discipline." (3B: 38) Church discipline for Löhe was chiefly a concern over who should be admitted to the Lord's Supper. "The principle, Lutheran altars only for Lutheran communicants, was to be enforced. Pastors were to exclude from the Sacrament members who obviously lacked faith, insisted upon rejecting the confessions, or lived in open sin, until they could be brought to repent... It was mixed altar fellowship in particular which burdened Löhe's conscience" (Ottersberg: 173–174) His personal opposition to the unionistic State Church brought him almost to the point of leaving to form a Lutheran Free Church. At one point he was actually suspended from the Bavarian State Church. But eventually, most of the demands made by Löhe and his confessional associates were accommodated. (cf. 3B: 38) The primary thing which Löhe did achieve was in fact the formal separation of the Lutheran and Reformed churches. "In 1853 a separate synod for the Reformed Church was established and for the first time the use of the title 'Lutheran' was made legal in Bavaria." (3B: 38n118) Löhe was, by and large, unsuccessful in his efforts to secure the adoption of strict confessional practice throughout the new Lutheran State Church in his day. (cf. Ottersberg: 173) But without a doubt, "Löhe's work contributed greatly to the victory of confessionalism in the Bavarian Church, which is today one of the strongest Lutheran Churches in the world." (3B: 39)[3]

Confessional Lutheran Identity:

Wilhelm Löhe's confessional Lutheran heritage, kindled in the context of the *Awakening* and proved in his struggles with the State Church, was for him not some "dead" orthodoxy nor a tradition preserved simply for the sake of tradition. Rather, for Löhe, confessional Lutheran orthodoxy is the vital and living source of the Church's mission. His identity as a Lutheran is no mere arbitrary preference for one equivalent denomination among many. He insisted that the Lutheran Church is *the* one denomination that holds faithfully to the Scriptures and "has the highest treasures of the Church unperverted" (3B: 113): "We admit that the so-called Lutheran Church is just one denomination, one part of the visible Church, but we also claim, despite some faults it may have, that it is nevertheless the one among all which has the mark of the pure denomination, the Church par excellence." (3B: 111)

> No one has yet been able to prove that our confessions are in error on one single point. It is still true that every simple reader who compares our distinctive doctrines with the clear words of the Holy Scriptures must confirm the truth of our confessions. The Augsburg Confession may be refuted by the writings of the fathers, which do not always agree, but it can never be refuted by God's Word. If the Lutheran Church has the pure Word and Sacrament in a pure confession, it obviously has the highest treasures of the Church unperverted. It thus has God's fullness and the living source from which all deficiencies may be supplied. (3B: 113)

---

3 For additional information, cf. Conser, "A Conservative Critique of Church and State."

For Löhe, confessional integrity is integrity to God's Word and to His truth. And this is important, not only for its own sake as a matter of faithfulness to God, but also for the sake of bringing people to salvation and maintaining the faith and salvation of those already in the Church. As Löhe writes:

> It is a difficult thing, possible only through divine power, to be saved where there is pure doctrine. How much harder it must be to be saved where error is mixed with truth! Love, which hopes all things, hopes that Baptism and portions of the truth can save even the members of impure denominations, but this is little more than a hope which persists when all other hopes have vanished. The closer we are to a man the more we wish that he might possess the complete truth and the entire fullness of the God–given means of grace and thus more easily come to eternal life. What we wish for others we must doubtless also wish for ourselves. (3B: 100–101)

And again:

> The Lutheran Church, because she maintains Word and Sacrament in its pure confession, is the fountain of truth—and out of her waters all others in other churches are satiated and made satisfied... From here issues all salvation, for here is unveiled—not partly—but completely as possible this side of the grave, the clear truth of the Gospel. That which other communities possess in the way of truth, is here united as The Truth. (Schober: 45–46)

Thus, for Löhe, not only is the pure doctrine of the Lutheran Church her greatest treasure, but to bear the light of that treasure before the world and all other denominations is her foremost duty. In his words:

> The greatest treasure of the Lutheran Church is the pure doctrine which flows from a pure confession. By virtue of this pure doctrine it has been and still is the center and source of the luminous sphere called Christendom. For three centuries the doctrine and life of all confessions have been purified by its witness, and there is no question that it has had and still

> has an influence on all who envy it. Even those who oppose it are made better by its light... To bear this cleansing, purifying witness in the midst of the confessions is the chief calling of the Church of God which is called Lutheran. (3B: 162)

In this way, Löhe considers the Lutheran Confessions to be the unifying center of the universal, catholic Church on earth.

> A disinterested and impartial comparison of Lutheran doctrine with the doctrines of other churches, especially those of the Roman and Reformed churches shows by analysis that the Lutheran Church is the rightful center between the two; that she is the *center of the confessions.* In not a single doctrine does she defend the extreme, but everywhere her doctrine offers the only possible union and unification of the completely fixed opposite extremes of those particular churches... The other confessions everywhere divide whereas the Lutheran doctrine everywhere shows unification and reconciliation of the truth contained in opposing statements. Never does our doctrine push isolated words of Scripture to extremes, but everywhere, by comparison of the apparently opposing statements, it has reached the Truth of God with beautiful form and limit. (Schober: 47)

Such statements on Löhe's part indicate his sincere appreciation for the true unity of the *Una Sancta* and his earnest desire to facilitate that unity on earth in the integrity of the one truth.

> In an age in which every third word is *union*, the children of the true Church therefore need to make it especially clear to themselves that their church, by virtue of the doctrine which she confesses, is the union of the two opposing viewpoints, and that it is the great calling of the pure Church to teach this true union and always to confront the opposing churches anew with it. [We must] prove that what everyone seeks is, when correctly understood, united in the doctrine of our Church and is brought to life through the living out of this teaching... The true Church prays without ceasing for the unification of all souls in the one true doctrine and hopes

that all sheep of the Good Shepherd will hear His voice in the proclamation of the true doctrine and gather themselves into one flock.[4]

Not only is the pure doctrine of the Lutheran Confessions the unifying center of all the other denominations of the Church; for Löhe, that pure doctrine is the source of unity also within the Lutheran Church, as well, and the key to accomplishing her work and mission. For example, Löhe writes in the conclusion of his *Three Books About the Church*:

> If once again in our time many are united in [the Confession of the Lutheran Church], if the confession of the fathers once again echoes in all Lutheran territories, if many extend the hand of brotherhood over land and sea and are openly united in preaching the holy truth of the Lutheran Church in all places and do not rest until all powers of body and soul have been used for the honor of this confession—what is there to keep us from believing that we stand in the dawn of its day of glory? The Lord is among us! Do we not notice it? Let us be united, brethren! Let our unity in the ancient truth and joy in the Lord be our strength! In love and sincerity let us worthily represent the holy church in the midst of the confessions! Let us recognize the task of our Church in missions and carry its torch into all the world! Let us be united! Let us be united before our people! One Word and doctrine, one practice of our ministers, one song of praise should be among us! Let us be zealous for unity! We have reason to be. (3B: 180)

Now it should be noted that, "while championing a return to the basis of the historic Lutheran Confessions, Löhe envisaged no simple repristination but rather a development of the Confessions; he looked for new forms of the Church, of church–state relations, of worship, of missionary and philanthropic work within the Lutheran Church." (Heintzen–1964: 1) Löhe looked for no *changes* in the confessional *doctrine*, but rather for that doctrine to be applied and

---

[4] Meyer, *Moving Frontiers: Readings in the History of the Lutheran Church—Missouri Synod*: 71. [Hereafter, cited in-line, according to the format: (MF: 71).]

practiced more fully in the life of the Church. As he writes:

> Perhaps one could also say that the reformation of doctrine has taken place; but the Church still does not rejoice in the riches of her pure doctrine as she should, and does not sense the significance which this gives her. She still feels as if she were only tolerated, as if she lived by the grace of men. She does not know that she has a letter of emancipation from God to live openly and freely by His grace and her faith and to make the whole world happy through her riches. She does not recognize that, after she became the pure Church, she became preeminently heir of all divine promises. She still thinks of herself too much as mere dogma, too little as a person; she is too little conscious of herself, her grace, her worth, her powers. In ecclesiastical consciousness, life, and work she is a long way from being again what the pure Church of the first centuries was! Here a Reformation is still needed! (MF: 70)

This attitude is undoubtedly behind Löhe's innovations of the "Practical Seminary" in Fort Wayne and the Deaconess Motherhouse in Neuendettelsau. He did hold a deep appreciation and respect for historical forms and traditions. As one biographer writes: "Löhe's preoccupation with the Church's tradition is an indication of... his marked sense of history. He pursued historical study with regularity and relish... He said: 'I am a great friend of historical study; next to the study of God's Word, I value it most.'" (Heintzen–1964: 30) But Löhe was no traditionalist. He saw the Gospel–given freedom in externals as an opportunity to carry out ever more thoroughly the implications of pure Lutheran doctrine in the Church's practice.

> Now that the pure, rich doctrine has been won, it is, however, necessary to fully apply it in all respects. Never yet has there been a time when [the Church] was fully conscious of her riches—when earnest consideration was given to the question of what all could be done with them for the welfare of the world and of the Church. ... Begin to search, to seek, and to find. One should not be too narrow–minded in holding fast certain forms and externals existing since the Reformation. Many a thesis remains without its antithesis, many an antith-

esis without its thesis. Many an abuse has been discarded with its pious use. Much has been discarded simply for polemical reasons. And it was not noted that what was discarded may be readopted when the polemic becomes superfluous. (MF: 70)

Löhe branded his theological position as "Sacramental Lutheranism," a term that adequately reflects his great love and appreciation for the Sacrament of the Altar. It was the Lord's Supper, in particular, which had sharpened his identity as a Lutheran *vis–á–vis* the Reformed, and it was the Lord's Supper which would continue throughout his life to give shape and definition to his Lutheranism. Concerning this Sacramental identity, he made the following remarks at a pastors' conference in 1865:

> I am the same good Lutheran as earlier, but in a more profound way. Before Lutheranism was for me little more than affirmation of the confessions from A–Z; now the whole of Lutheranism is for me hidden in the Sacrament of the Altar, in which, as can be shown, all the chief doctrines of Christianity, especially those of the Reformation, have their center and focus. The essential thing for me now is not so much the Lutheran doctrine of the Lord's Supper, but sacramental life and the experience of the blessings of the Sacrament possible only through partaking of it abundantly. The words "sacramental Lutheranism" signify my advance. (Schattauer, "Sunday Worship": 371n2)

Certainly, it was never Löhe's intention to depart from the pure doctrine of his beloved Lutheran Church, as he indicates so very clearly in the brief Latin autobiography that he wrote in the official ordination book on the day before his ordination:

> The Augsburg Confession, if such an unworthy one as I may be permitted to say so, is also my confession, and the rest of the symbolical books of the Evangelical Lutheran Church, agreeing with the Augustana, are also *norma normata* for me. Those persons who are opposed to this faith of ours I do not hate... Certainly I hate no one, but from the bottom of my heart I do hate all pernicious doctrines of men and condemn

what the Augsburg Confession rejects. By God's help I shall preach the true doctrine and not be silent until the Lord himself take me, his peace–loving soldier, out of the church militant into the blessed quietude of the church triumphant! (3B: 6–7)[5]

Three Books About the Church:

In all that Wilhelm Löhe did, he was and remained above all else a man of the Church. "The uniting center" of his ministry, his liturgical theology, and of all his mission efforts "was his struggle for the [earthly] form and life of the true believing Church." (Schober: 41) And for this dear Church he has the greatest, undying love, obvious in his description of Her:

> The Church consists of the community founded by God and the union of predestined souls united with each other and with Him. In her resides the love that is well pleasing to God and transfigures all other love. The Church is the most beautiful thought of God in which His own love for humanity toward His Son manifests itself with veiled face. God's most beautiful glory is love. In the Church, love piled up beyond measure reveals itself to all members—the living, the dying, the redeemed—from now through all eternity! (Schober: 41)

It is not surprising, therefore, that one of Löhe's most profound and lasting works is his *Three Books About the Church*. Here he articulates his thoughts on the question that more than any other attracted the attention of the newly "awakened" confessional Lutherans; namely, "What is the Church?" (3B: 33)[6]

Pastor Löhe first began consideration of his *Three Books About the Church* in 1843, when visited by F. C. D. Wyneken, who at that time expressed his personal interest in such a treatment of the Church for use among the German Lutherans in America. "Apparently, how-

---

5 For additional information on Löhe's Confessional Lutheran identity, cf. Weis, *The Place of the Lutheran Confessions in Lutheranism Past and Present*.

6 "He represents well an emerging churchly consciousness and the desire that the visible structures of church life, especially the liturgy, be taken seriously as the means for shaping and expressing ecclesial life" (Schattauer, "Sunday Worship": 372).

ever, Löhe gave no more attention to the project until late that year. On All Saints' Day he spoke at a prayer service on the subject of the church triumphant. The same afternoon he walked with his wife to a neighboring village, and on the way she told him what meaning his words had had for her." (3B: 36–37) Löhe writes in his diary: "We dwelt upon the thought that the Church is like a long procession of pilgrims whose first members are already in Zion while the rest still travel down here. How I enjoyed it with her. " (3B: 37)

It was only 24 days later that his dear wife, Helene, was called to join the host already in Zion. Earlier that same year, Helene's best friend and Helene's mother had died; and less than a year later, Löhe's infant son, Philip, also died. There can be little doubt that these events were the impetus behind the actual composition of *Three Books About the Church*. "The loss of his loved ones is clearly seen in what is almost an otherworldly preoccupation of Löhe's work." (3B: 37) For example, Löhe writes:

> To me it is such a joyous thought that I am not alone, that I do not travel by myself, but that I am accompanied on my pilgrimage through the valley of the shadow by a communion of believers. Right in the midst of this life's barren wilderness this thought can dissolve all sorrow in forgetfulness. Yet this communion of saints is not a mere thought but is an unshakable certainty. I know from the mouth of God that I am not alone... I see round about me right here so many men—both close friends and associates—whom I have good reason to accept as children of God. It is true that I do not know with divine assurance, but with almost absolute certainty, that this one or that one of my friends is a child of God, won from all eternity. I rejoice over this from the bottom of my heart, but unfortunately my joy is not unmixed with sorrow, for death takes away many a soul I love. Like candles, one after another in the bright circle of my friends goes out, the empty places turn dark, and seldom does another star fill the dark void. This brings pain and longing. Yet I do not forget that these brethren of whom I speak are just hidden from my sight and have been placed in higher positions in the kingdom of God... Those who live in the Lord and those who, while out of

the body, abide in him; those who are still pilgrims and those who are already home; those who walk by faith and those who walk by sight—these are not two separated flocks, but one, one before God and one according to their own consciousness. (3B: 51–52)

These events are mentioned, not only because *Three Books About the Church* is such an important aspect of Löhe's life and ministry, but also because the thoughts expressed in this great work, and the events prompting its creation, are integral to Löhe's life–long burning zeal for missions.

Motivation For Missions:

In *missions*, Wilhelm Löhe found the natural result of all that was most important to him. Insistence on pure doctrine took Löhe ever back to the pure center of all doctrines—Christ and His universal atonement for *all men*. He criticizes the false doctrine of double–predestination because it denies this universal grace of God in Christ, and because it can therefore easily "cripple all desire to reach the nations with God's Gospel." By contrast, knowing that Christ has atoned for all men, and that He now sincerely calls all men to faith, "makes us zealous in calling the heathen, for God calls through the office of preaching." Löhe writes: "It is amazing how much in the doctrine of the Church and its activity (mission) depends on the doctrine of universal grace." (3B: 81–84) Understanding the Lutheran Church as the purest expression of the Church universal meant for Löhe that she also has the greatest responsibility to shine forth with the Gospel. His great comfort and encouragement in all of this is God's promise of eternity; the reality of the Church Triumphant.

Löhe found his motivation for missions also in his great love for the Sacrament of the Altar. For Löhe, this Holy Supper is the center of the Church's entire life and activity. And as the Lord and Savior comes to His Church in loving condescension with His precious Body and Blood, so does His Body the Church come with the Gospel to all the heathen. In fact, in his biography of Wilhelm Löhe, Theodor Schober comments beautifully that for Löhe, "the perpetually new movement of the church back to the one and only source—Christ, is at the same time an urge into the distance beyond all borders of land and confession." He then goes on to cite from *Three Books About the Church* one of Löhe's most oft-quoted comments: "Mission is nothing other than the Church of God in action!" (Schober: 43)

> The Church of the New Testament is no longer a territorial church but a Church of all people, a Church which has its children in all lands and gathers them from every nation. It is the one flock of the one Shepherd, called out of many folds (John 10:16), the universal—the truly catholic—Church which flows through all time and into which all people pour. This is the great concept which is still being fulfilled, the work of God in the final hour of the world, the dearest thought of all the saints in life and in death, the thought for which they lived and still live, died and still die. This is the thought which must permeate the mission of the Church or it will not know what it is or what it should do. For mission is nothing but the one Church of God in motion, the actualization of the one universal, catholic Church. Wherever mission enters in, the barriers which separate nation from nation fall down. Wherever it comes it brings together what previously was far off and widely separated. Wherever it takes root it produces that wonderful unity which makes "the people of every tongue" able to understand one another in all things. Mission is the life of the catholic Church. Where it stops, blood and breath stop; where it dies, the love which unites heaven and earth also dies. The catholic Church and mission—these two no one can separate without killing both, and that is impossible. (3B: 59)

As will be clearly seen, Löhe's motivation for missions was realized in action. As James L. Schaaf reflects, on the basis of one of Löhe's missionary sermons, in his introduction to Löhe's *Three Books About the Church*:

> The force that drove this simple pastor of Neuendettelsau was nothing more than the desire to spread the gospel to all lands, to obey the missionary command of Christ. When appeals from people who needed the Word of God came to him,

whether from America or from somewhere closer to home, he had to answer. In all that he did, in Neuendettelsau or in the farthest corner of the earth, Löhe was a missionary. (3B: 26)

LÖHE'S MISSION AND MINISTRY WITHIN HIS CONGREGATION:

Pstor Löhe's love for the Church as the community of God's own people was obvious in his pastoral ministry at Neuendettelsau. Here he could practice the confessional Lutheran orthodoxy that he so strongly desired for the whole Church. He concentrated on solid, Biblical preaching in particular (a rarity in the age of Rationalism) and on faithful pastoral care of his flock. He preached his sermons in the context of dignified, reverent and historically-sound liturgical settings. And throughout his ministry, he stressed the Church's sacramental life, a thorough catechesis of young and old, the visitation and nurture of the sick, and the use of Private Confession and brotherly discipline (cf. Ottersberg: 176). In giving advice to younger, novice pastors, Löhe reveals his "rule of thumb" for pastoral ministry:

> Use the old means in the old way and continue in instruction, learning, experience, in temptation and prayer, so that you will ripen into a real pastor! You will be able to come close to your parishioners both publicly and separately, but do not in any way over do it with any kind of means or gifts! Simply do your part! Prayerfully use the ancient means when circumstance is suitable, and let God do the worrying as to the outcome! You may make house visits and again not, visit the sick when called and at times when not called, do this or that, and again do it not, just as you find it to be best under the existing circumstances after quiet consideration before God. But do not make anything a fetter upon you and a load upon your conscience! (Schober: 67)

Already during his vicarages, Löhe had distinguished himself as a powerful preacher of God's Word. (3B: 7–8) And he maintained his reputation as such throughout his ministry at Neuendettelsau. In fact, Löhe's "reputation as a pulpit force was recognized far beyond the countryside of Neuendettelsau... He had an appeal which attracted peasants from miles around as well as city dwellers of Fuerth and Nuremberg who came on foot Sundays to Neuendettelsau to hear him preach." (Heintzen–1964: 27) His success was surely due in part to his high estimation of preaching as the primary "means which the Church uses for the salvation of souls." (3B: 167)

> Among the means which the church uses for the salvation of souls, preaching occupies the first place. It is the means for calling those who are far off and for confirming the call and election of those who have been called and have drawn near. In preaching the Church does not think it necessary to support the holy Word by human artifice. The important thing is not to hinder its power and effectiveness and not to impose any sort of method upon the Word which does not befit it. The preacher proclaims salvation in Jesus Christ with the consciousness that it is not anything he adds but the precious contents of the Word itself which will separate souls from the world and bring them close to God. (3B: 167)

In keeping with his high estimation of preaching, Löhe *worked* to develop and hone his homiletical skills. As a younger man, he studied especially the published sermons of noted preachers, with emphasis on Luther in particular, as well as men like Chrysostom and Savonarola. (cf. Ottersberg: 177) It should also be noted that, during his semester at the University of Berlin, Löhe was exposed to the preaching of Friedrich Schleiermacher. And while he did not especially appreciate the *content* of either Schleiermacher's sermons or his lectures, he was greatly influenced by his homiletical style, which he later emulated in his own preaching. (cf. 3B: 6) Later in life, he broadened his reading to include a wide variety of things: "periodicals, theological works in all branches, literature, history." (Ottersberg: 177) And though his preaching was always *Biblical*, his sermons also reflected his broad literary background. Ultimately, a number of factors combined to make Löhe an effective preacher: "He knew the Bible thoroughly; he expounded it lucidly; he used vivid language. He had the ability to adapt his sermon to the needs of his hearers. His resonant voice and commanding physical appearance likewise contributed to the effectiveness of his presentation. Behind it all lay painstaking preparation." (Heintzen–1964: 27) As Löhe writes: "With suffering must I bring forth my sermons. From Monday until Sunday I work during the first hours of the day on the sermon. I sigh, pray, and fear until I mount the pulpit—and then God's grace is made new." (Heintzen–1964: 27)

Though Löhe was an accomplished preacher, who did indeed place "considerable weight on the sermon in public worship" (Heintzen–1964: 28), he also stressed the role of the liturgy, as well. In fact, in a letter to one of his American missionaries he mentions his hope "that he would be able to adjust his congregation to the perfect harmony of the Lutheran service and in so doing that prevent the whole sanctuary from shriveling into the sermon." (Greenholt: 7) This was in part a reaction to the forces of Rationalism that had been neglecting the liturgy for many years. (cf. Ottersberg: 178) But Löhe had been a student of the liturgy already from his youth, and so it was "a subject to which he devoted his time happily and profitably." (Schaaf–1961: 79)[7] Indeed, as a pastor, "The hours spent leading his congregation in worship were precious ones for Löhe. 'In the worship services,' he wrote, 'the congregation feels itself closest to its Lord. There as close to the Bridegroom as it can get, it leads a heavenly life on earth, an earthly life in heaven.'" (3B: 15)

Though Löhe was wholly un–musical, in the liturgy he was clearly at home in element. As one of his closest associates at Neuendettelsau, Ernst Lotze, describes:

> Löhe was a great lover of aesthetics; in music he was a perfect layman, he was completely unable to carry a tune, yet his liturgical speaking sounded like music... When he stepped to the Altar in the midst of the congregation it could clearly be seen: Here is the life substance of this man; here he is at home. Therefore, he was able without effort and without aiming at it to bring the entire congregation to a solemn devotion. (Schober: 82–83)

---

7 "The rich collection of Lutheran church orders and prayer books which filled his library in the humble parsonage assisted the eager, learned scholar at the same time to become an exceptional classical liturgist" (Schober: 83)."

For all his deep appreciation of the liturgy, Löhe never foisted anything upon his congregation. Instead, by patient catechesis, he taught his people liturgy. "Only after ten years did he introduce the full form of the Lutheran communion liturgy in his congregation." (Heintzen–1964: 28) "Through training and instruction he welded the members of his congregation into a group which participated in the services with such unison that one visitor of rank to his church said: 'You have a liturgical people.'" (Greenholt: 8)[8] And this in a parish of simple, peasant people, "rather stolid and set in their ways"! Lotze describes the situation:

> [The culminating point] in the life of the congregation... were the church services in that insignificant little church. The week–day services, Wednesday and Friday were complete, the Sunday services were brimful, organ music certainly, song, mighty liturgy complete and classical... The peasants sang powerfully, harsh and coarse, often in a dialect. Yet, with all that there existed an inexorable seriousness; a fervor so powerful that the aesthetically–trained ear was able to put up with everything willingly, and, for the sake of the essential, overlook the insignificant outward things. (Schober: 83–84)

Soon after coming to Neuendettelsau, Löhe began an intensive study of historical liturgies. And the idea was in his mind for some time to produce his own orders of service faithfully based on the historic Lutheran agenda. As with his *Three Books About the Church*, what prompted Löhe finally to go ahead with this idea was a request from F. C. D. Wyneken and the earliest of Löhe's American missionaries for a German order of service to be used by Lutheran congregations in America.[9] This request—coupled with the

---

8 "One time when Lotze was privileged to take the great Lutheran D. Uhlhorn from Hannover through Neuendettelsau and then accompany him to Heilsbronn; in parting that man said: 'above all else do I envy you for your church services; I have never heard anything to equal that.'" (Schober: 83)

9 [9]Löhe dedicated the First Edition of the *Agende* to Wyneken, as follows:
> To Friedrich Wyneken in St. Louis, Missouri. I have dedicated this agenda to you, dear friend and brother. For this work has been done in a spirit of genuine love for my brothers in North America, of whom you were the

fact that Löhe found consolation in his liturgical studies following his bereavement—resulted in Löhe's *Agende fuer christliche Gemeinden des lutherischen Bekenntnisses* in 1844.[10]

Reflecting his sense and appreciation of the one, holy, catholic, and apostolic Church in all times and places, Löhe's *Agende* is the product of extensive liturgical studies, involving more than 200 older forms of worship. These forms included the Lutheran Church Orders of the Reformation period, the ancient and medieval liturgies, the Roman missal, and the Anglican *Book of Common Prayer*. Löhe "became particularly interested in the liturgies of the old eastern churches." (Ottersberg: 179) As a result, the *Agende* is a masterpiece of both liturgical and historical scholarship, and without a doubt the most cross–cultural agenda for worship ever produced. In Löhe's mind, nothing was "too good for his beloved church at worship." (3B: 15) His aim was to complete, correct, and supplement wherever needed the form of the Divine Service by means of Eastern and pre–Reformation liturgies. However, partly as an exercise of self–discipline, and partly out of pastoral concern for the weaker brethren, Löhe refrained from including in the liturgy of his *Agende* anything which had not already been employed in one of the old Lutheran Orders.

Though the *Agende* was intended specifically for the Lutheran missions in America, it also accomplished a "resurgence of interest in liturgies in the Lutheran Church." (Ottersberg: 179) In fact,

> first to share with me the blessed work of love — the building of God's Zion across the ocean. Please joyfully receive this work as well as my sincerest, respectful greeting! (Löhe, *Prayer*)

10 The circumstances under which both the *Agende* and the *Three Books About the Church* were produced no doubt helped to foster Löhe's love for and understanding of liturgical worship as an activity of the Church—the worship, prayer, and confession of God's people, in which the pilgrim church on earth joins with the angels and archangels and all the host of heaven. In the liturgy, Löhe found himself as close as possible on this side of the grave to his dear Helene, to his father and his son, and to all his other loved ones lost to death. All of these and countless others joined with him to worship the source of their everlasting life together: the Lamb upon His Throne. He writes in the preface to his *Agende*:

> With this Great Prayer [of the Church in the Divine Service] the thought comes to them, that the Church on earth and the Church in Heaven is the One Holy Catholic Church, and that the prayers of the pilgrims here and the prayers of the glorified there, are borne to the Father's Throne by the same Mediator. (Löhe, *Liturgy for Christian Congregations*: xv.)

Löhe's *Agende* "was a guide in the recovery of the Lutheran ritual which culminated in the Common Service." (Greenholt: 256) It was used in the Missouri Synod for a number of years. And "as late as 1919 a revised edition was published by the Iowa Synod for use in its congregations." (Schaaf–1961: 80) It would no doubt seem quite familiar to those accustomed to modern Lutheran hymnals. The chief component of the *Agende* is "The Service with Holy Communion, to which are added the orders for Matins and Vespers and a number of occasional services such as baptisms, funerals, and marriages. The work also contains a rich selection of prayers and collects and information about the Church Year." (Schaaf–1961: 80)[11]

Löhe's Theology of Liturgical Worship:

Löhe himself provides the best and certainly the most eloquent summary of his thoughts on the liturgy in one of the final chapters of his *Three Books About the Church*. By virtue of its lasting merit and the special insight it provides into Löhe's liturgical theology, his chapter on the liturgy will provide the basic outline and much of the substance for the discussion of Löhe as a confessional Lutheran liturgiologist.[12]

Liturgy as Prayer

Löhe defines the liturgy most simply as a prayer: the corporate prayer of the Church: "The Church is not only an assembly that learns but also an assembly that prays. It prays not only as individual members in their closets but also together as large gatherings in its houses of assembly." (3B: 176)[13] There is for Löhe an intentional continuity

---

11 For an English translation of Löhe's *Agende*, cf. the recently reprinted *Liturgy for Christian Congregations of the Lutheran Faith*. Citations herein are taken from this English translation, which will nevertheless be designated by the German "*Agende*" whenever referenced.

12 A definitive work on Löhe's liturgical theology, regrettably available only in German, is Hans Kressel's *Wilhelm Löhe als Liturg und Liturgiker* (Neuendettelsau: Freimund, 1952). cf. Schattauer, "Sunday Worship": 374n8.

13 [13] Löhe writes, "The Church in which the Name of the Lord Jesus is preached and the congregation gathers for prayer has a great blessing. All the Christians

between individual and corporate prayer. Thus, for example, he writes in his *Agende*, "the liturgical hours of the day, morning, noon and evening, are announced by the prayer–bell, and kept with prayer by the people, whether at home or abroad." (*Agende*: 5) In the Preface to his popular *Seed–Grains of Prayer*, Löhe makes clear his intention that family devotions should follow liturgical form and be connected to the worship of the Church. The "regulation of family worship" is "patterned after the example of the daily matins and vesper services of the Church, or after other acceptable rubrics" (Löhe, *Seed–Grains*: 73). Prayers in the home are united to the Church's prayer especially by their sanctification of time through a participation in the liturgical ebb and flow of hours, days, and weeks throughout the Church Year. Accordingly, *Seed–Grains of Prayer* is arranged according to morning, daily, and evening prayers, the Christian week, and the Church Year.[14] Another prayer book, *Essential Prayers for the Home—Christian Prayers for those of The Augsburg Confession*, is designed for us as an home "agenda," and "for all intents and purposes, this book could have functioned as a daily office for the home." As described in *Seed–Grains* and elsewhere, the cycle of the book of *Essential Prayers* should be filled with one Spirit and the praying shepherd should merely be the voice of his flock. The community prayer of the Church is a one and single great blessedness" (Schober: 77).

14 In his *Seed–Grains of Prayer*, Löhe remarks on how "a Christian lives his days with Christ and in contemplation of Him."

> His *Days* pass in remembering the sufferings of Jesus. When the clock strikes eleven, he knows that the bells are ringing in the noon hour of his Redeemer, when thick darkness overshadowed Him. In the afternoon at three o'clock, he breathes a grateful prayer of joy, for the Lord has finished. Every stroke of the clock calls upon him to consider what Christ did and suffered in that hour.
>
> His *Weeks* are pictures of Christ's life. Sunday, at each return, is the brother of Easter Day, the most joyful day of the week. It is preceeded by days of repentance and suffering. Wednesday already brings the memory of the unholy bargaining of Judas with the high priests and murders of Christ. Thursday divides the mind between the struggles in Gethsemane and the blessed institution of the Lord's Supper. Every Friday is a weekly "Good Friday." Every Saturday is a sabbath of the rest of Christ in the grave.
>
> As is the week so also the *Year*: It recalls the life, suffering, and death of the Christ, an ever new experience of what the gospels narrate: itself a very gospel of Christ our Lord. (Löhe, *Seed–Grains*: 433)

"is based upon the daily turn of the hours, the change of the seasons, the church year, the spiritual [Sacramental] life, and the home life." (Löhe, *Prayer*) Elsewhere, Löhe writes, "Important is the exercise [of prayer] from Church to the home and closet and from the closet and home to the Church." (Schober: 75)

Liturgical Freedom

Löhe's refusal to foist a fuller liturgy immediately upon his congregation is practical evidence for his balanced, *Lutheran* understanding of externals. He refers to *Augustana* VII in the preface to his *Agende*, citing as "perhaps the greatest word of that document" that "it is sufficient for the true unity of the Church, that the Gospel is preached therein according to its pure intent and meaning, and that the Sacraments are administered in conformity with the Word of God," and that "for the true unity of the Christian Church it is not necessary that uniform ceremonies, instituted by men, should be everywhere observed." (*Agende*: x) Clearly, Löhe recognized and was adamant to insist that the outward trappings of the Church *do not make* her what she is.

> We protest against the idea of an *opus operatum* and an overestimation of externals. The church remains what it is even without the liturgy. It remains a queen, even if dressed in beggar's rags. It would be better if everything else were lost and only the pure doctrine remained safe than for us to continue the ceremony and adornment of glorious services which lack the light and life because the doctrine has become impure. (3B: 178)

> Further I say, and without fear of contradiction, that Constitutions and Organizations, Liturgies and Ceremonies, valuable in the service of the truth as they may be, do not in the real sense constitute the Church. From these the Church does not derive its life; they are fruits of its life, but not its source. It is gratifying to the enemy, and humiliating to the devout, to see many over–estimate the value of externals, thus going the way of Rome... The holy Church of God is a miracle of its one

Lord and Head, and shows itself perpetually independent of all that is not Word and Sacrament. (*Agende*: ix.–x.)

Thus, Löhe fully recognized that liturgical forms are largely *adiaphora*, neither commanded nor forbidden by God. At the same time, however, he also believed that the Church's freedom in *adiaphora* should not become anarchy. "Constitutions and Liturgies are subordinate; but in preparing them for the use of the Church, it becomes us to seek everywhere for that which is edifying and commendable." (*Agende*: x.) In any case, the Church in the course of her history has utilized not just any form but carefully selected forms that adequately express her doctrine and carry her worship: "[The] forms are free. Few of them are commanded. Yet despite this freedom, from its very beginning the Church has been pleased to select certain forms. A holy variety of singing and praying has grown up and a lovely pattern of approach to, and withdrawal from, the Lord of lords has been established." (3B: 177)

Liturgical Form

Löhe insists that freedom in the use of liturgical forms must be exercised with extreme caution. New forms should not be established by anyone who has not yet been instructed by the old, lest he permit the Church to become a sect formed in his own image. The old forms have much to offer, and "where they aren't broken, they shouldn't be 'fixed'."

> We must beware of misusing our liturgical freedom to produce new liturgies. One should rather use the old forms and learn to understand and have a feeling for them before one feels oneself competent to create something new and better. He who has not tested the old cannot create something new. It is a shame when everybody presumes to form his own opinions about hymns and the liturgy without having thoroughly looked into the matter. Let a man first learn in silence and not act as if it were a matter of course that he understands everything! Once a man has first learned from the old he can profitably use the developments of recent times (in language and methods

of speech) for the benefit of the liturgy. (3B: 178)

As already demonstrated in the case of the *Agende*, no one followed Löhe's exhortation to learn from the old more thoroughly than Löhe himself. And on the basis of his extensive research, he lays out in the Preface to his *Agende* a winsome point–by–point explanation of the Lutheran Order of Divine Service. Much can be learned about Löhe's liturgical theology by reviewing his discussion of these individual parts of the Church's worship.

By way of introduction, Löhe sets the parameters of worship in relation to the Word and Sacrament: specifically, the Sermon and the Holy Communion. As divinely-ordained means of grace, these two aspects of liturgical worship are *not adiaphora*; they are not free. While the *particular* form of liturgical worship remains free, the very nature of the Divine Service as determined by Word and Sacrament makes the use of some order quite necessary. The Divine Service is no more random in its progression than the *ordo salutus*: "Word and Sacrament determine the order of salvation, and this determines the order of the Divine Service. Just as spiritual life without the order of salvation is unthinkable, so a Divine Service without order, without a scriptural progression of salutary thought is unimaginable." (Löhe, *Prayer*) Consequently, an appropriate liturgy must conform to the shape of worship established by the means of grace. The congregation—and so also her Divine Service—are formed and shaped by the dynamic activity of Word and Sacrament; therefore, liturgical worship is hardly to be an arbitrary event, but must reflect this well–spring of the Church's life.

> The congregation, in her inner life and in her Divine Service, stands like a craggy rock in the midst of the Sea of Word and Sacrament. Like the sea surges against the cliff, so the blessed forms of the Liturgy wash the congregation with the precious truths of either the Word or the Sacrament. As the sea rises up and breaks forth upon the jagged rocks, so that the breaking wave and the spray is caused by the rocks, even so the liturgical life is no mere arbitrary occurrence, rather it wells forth from the innermost source of spiritual existence, the Word and the Sacraments, as they break forth upon the

congregation. (Löhe, *Prayer*)

In this way, the Divine Service is comprised of twin mountain peaks, like Mt. Horeb and Mt. Sinai in the Old Testament: the sermon, as the first and lower of the two pinnacles, and the Sacrament of the Altar as the apex of the Service. It hardly needs to be added that for Löhe a service without the celebration of the Lord's Supper is sorely lacking.[15]

In public worship the soul is engaged in an ascent, the goal of which is reached at the Table of the Lord, than which there is nothing higher—nothing diviner on earth, only Heaven remains above. In the Holy Supper the deepest longings of the soul are satisfied, as the humble worshiper joyfully declares in the Nunc Dimittis. (*Agende*: xii.)[16]

---

15 It is true that Löhe did provide for an Order of Morning Service without Communion (cf. *Agende*: 47ff.); he inherited a pattern of Eucharistic celebration which entailed all of two seasonal periods during which the Lord's Supper would be offered for a series of Sundays. Typically, the members would partake of the Sacrament once per season! Löhe worked from this point rather quickly to the celebration of the Lord's Supper on a tri–weekly basis, and eventually he offered the Sacrament every week by using a "small Communion" service prior to the regular Morning Service on "non–Communion" Sundays (cf. Schattauer, "Sunday Worship": 378). Löhe's deep disatisfaction with the previous *status quo* may be inferred in the note he included at the end of his Morning Service without Communion:

> A morning service on Sundays or Festivals without the Communion is like a broken column. If a Communion has been announced on a previous Sunday, and none present themselves to receive, it is evidence that the spiritual life of the congregation is in a wretched condition. On such occasions the congregation is to be admonished, at the conclusion of the sermon, of the necessity of desiring earnestly the best treasures. For this purpose I append the following Exhortation... (*Agende*: 54)

The Exhortation itself has the flavor of Luther's "Brief Exhortation to Confession" at the close of the Large Catechism. It reads in part:

> Now we say, We are rich, and increased with goods, and have need of nothing; therefore we do not receive what He offers, nor come when He invites. Hence it is not surprising that we are wretched, poor, blind and naked, full of sin, burdened with an evil conscience, and without desire to do good. (*Agende*: 55)

16 Löhe's emphasis on the Lord's Supper as the pinnacle of the Divine Service reflects his own holy awe and awareness of God's presence in the Sacrament.

> Anyone who had ever witnessed Löhe at the Altar could not help but be most deeply impressed. "His soul rose up flame–like. The 'Holy, Holy,

Löhe proceeds to demonstrate that, just as the Lutheran Church in her public Confession teaches Word and Sacrament purely and correctly, so also is the Lutheran Order of Divine Service in perfect harmony with these means of grace. Löhe's demonstration, however, is not cast in the style of polemic or apologetic; it simply sets forth in positive, devotional terms the meaning of the various parts of the Lutheran liturgy.[17]

- *The Confiteor and Absolution.* The Confession and Absolution are the forms of approach unto God and of preparation for coming into His presence.

  The Christian desires to draw near to God in humble, acceptable worship. He comes, in company with his fellow Christians, from the conflicts of the past week, bearing on his heart the burdens of many defeats and the joys of few victories. He knows, that in spite of his best efforts his conduct has not been wholly pleasing to God. Before him lies now a new week with its thousand hopes and fears; and before he dares enter upon this new week, he must hold communion with God his heavenly Father. But how shall he approach his God who dwells in unapproachable light? First of all he must be pardoned of his sins, and be made sensible of such pardon. For this purpose there is no form better adapted than that given in this Liturgy for Confession and Absolution. (*Agende*: xii.–xiii.)

Holy' of Isaiah 6 had been given him as a special Word of God at his ordination. Hence he prayed at the Altar in the presence of God and the holy angels. In their presence he celebrated Holy Communion. The angelic forms in gallery of the Deaconess church in Neuendettelsau call to memory the presence of the Holy Majesty (Friederich Hansz)." (Schober: 82)

17 Löhe makes the same point in his Catechism. Having defined the true Church as "that which teaches and confesses God's Word purely, and administers the Sacraments according to the institution of Christ," Löhe indicates that the Lutheran Church meets these criteria. Her teachings may be known "from her confessions, which no Lutheran preacher dare contradict"; and her administration of the Sacraments can be discovered "from the Liturgies, which no pastor dare disregard" (Löhe, *Questions and Answers*: 106).

- *The Introit*. The *Introit* marks the congregation's entry into the presence of God; it also defines the character of the day within its liturgical context.

  The worshiper is now prepared to enter upon the meaning and character of the particular day, which are announced to him in the Introit. To the peace, experienced in hearing the Absolution, are thus added the joys of the particular festival. The Introit distinguishes one Lord's day from another. (*Agende*: xiii.)

- *The Kyrie*. The *Kyrie* is not another confession of sins, *per se*; it is a confession of *need* and a petition for God, as the Maker and Ruler of all, to look with mercy and compassion on the needs of His people.[18]

  Being cleansed from sin, and having entered upon the peculiar joys of the particular festival, the worshiper finds that earth has still other burdens and sorrows which prove a present and future hindrance to holiness. Life, death and eternity, upon each of which sin has cast its dark shadow, are things well able to make the soul tremble whenever it contemplates them. To be cleansed from the sins of the past week is no assurance of immunity from failure for the next. Therefore the Kyrie, comprehending, in spite of its brevity, a prayer for temporal and eternal deliverance, comes next in the Order. (*Agende*: xiii.)

  To substitute, with moderns, the Kyrie for a Confiteor and the Gloria for an Absolution is forced and perverted in the extreme. As little as a beggar, with his 'Be so kind to help me,' thinks of saying that he is a sinner, can the Church use the Kyrie as a confession of sins. Not sin, but need is confessed. Even in the later versions of the Kyrie where the mention of sin occurs, sin is regarded in the sense of need. (*Agende*: 39)

---

18 "With the Hebrew words such as Amen, Hallelujah, Hosanna, the Church has also retained the use of the Greek Kyrie eleison, thus showing that there is throughout the world only one holy Catholic Church" (*Agende*: 40).

- *The Gloria and Collect*. The *Gloria* provides the angelic announcement of God's presence among the congregation of His people. Then, in recognition of that gracious presence of God, the people gather into a single petition a Collect for all their needs.[19]

  As the Lord first came to His people in the chorus of angels, so does He *now* make His first approach to the worshiping congregation in the lofty strains of the Gloria in Excelsis. He has come, but as yet He is silent; but the light of His countenance shines upon His people, and His ear is open to their prayers. Once more, therefore, the congregation frames all its needs into a single petition, and unitedly present it to the divine Throne in the Collect; and in clear comprehension of the common need of all, the people answer with a believing Amen. (*Agende*: xiii.–xiv.)

- *The Word of God*. After having thus far been silent, God now speaks directly to His people through His Apostolic Word in the Epistle and the Gospel.

  Up to this point the Lord has been silent, but *now* He speaks, and it becomes all flesh to be silent before Him. He grants the people the grace of His Word, but first in the Apostolic

---

[19] With reference to Collects, Löhe provides the following introductory notes: The derivation of the word Collect is uncertain. Whether it is to be understood as the prayer fo the collected congregation, or as the *Collecta*, i.e., the summary of all those things for which God ought to be petitioned, is a question which I am willing to let others determine. But whichever way it is taken, the Collect is that prayer of the congregation which comprehends in a single sentence or petition all those things, which the congregation believes to be necessary for its welfare on a particular day or under particular circumstances. A single petition, addressed to God the Father, in the Name of the only begotten Son, as the Son Himself commanded; a single sigh from the congregation direct to the Father's heart, and a single word concerning which all are agreed, this is the Collect; and the more it comprehends of this definition, the more it is a Collect. The Collects of the early Christians are in this respect simply glorious. (*Agende*: 61)

writings. For this grace the people express their praise in the Hallelujah and Gradual. But the Lord speaks again. This time ipsissima verba (His very words) in the Gospel. The Holy One is coming ever nearer to His own, and they answer Him with a joyful Laus Tibi, Christe! (*Agende*: xiv.)

- *The Credo.* Having heard the Word of God—and on the basis of that Word—the congregation now confesses the Creed as an expression of her confidence in the gracious presence of God.

The worship has developed to that point in which the congregation is now conscious of its union with the Lord, which it expresses in the Credo. No more the burdens of sin, no more the fear of evil, no more the sighs of longing, but joyful confidence fills every soul. (*Agende*: xiv.)

- *The Sermon.* The Sermon is the first pinnacle of the Divine Service, unveiling and expressing more fully the presence of God with His people.

The face of the Highest is unveiled in the Sermon, which in a high sense expresses the communion of the saints, all of whom are glad in the presence of God. Now the congregation stands on the first height of the Mountain of God, with the face turned still higher, even to the Sacrament. (*Agende*: xiv.)

- *The Offertory.* The Offertory signifies the living sacrifice of the people of God. It is the response of faith on the part of those who know themselves to be in fellowship with God.[20]

---

20 Löhe includes in his *Seed–Grains of Prayer* a rather lengthy prayer of "sacrifice and consecration unto God," to be used "during Communion, and at other times" (Löhe, *Seed–Grains*: 161). It recaptures and articulates well a Lutheran understanding of the priestly sacrifice of all believers; at the same time, by the clarity of its language, the prayer excludes any notion of the Romish sacrifice of the Mass. [At the risk of editorializing, it is the author's opinion that more emphasis on the eucharistic sacrifice would be a most salutary leaven in the Lutheran Church today. It would serve to remind the people of God that their "celebration" in this life is always under the Cross.]

> The worshiping people now know themselves as the Bride of the Lord; their hearts' longings are satisfied in Him and through Him; but not only through Him, also through fellowship with one another; they are the people of God—a unit in their inner life and experience. (*Agende*: xiv.–xv.)

As the people of God—secure in the knowledge that He is their God—the congregation offers its eucharistic sacrifices of prayer and self–surrender.

> By no means do we countenance the Romish idea of sacrifice. But it is correct and liturgically necessary that the people regard their praying and giving as sacrificial acts, according to the Scriptures. As long as the congregation does not regard its praying and giving as acts of sacrifice—truly only of praise and thanksgiving,—it is but natural to find that its praying and giving are of a very desultory and meagre sort. The Offertory is a devotional act of the universal priesthood of believers. (*Agende*: 41–42)

- *The Prayers of the Church.* The Prayers of the Church are a continuation of the priestly sacrifice. Now the people of God offer their supplication, prayer, and intercession for all mankind.[21]

> In the fullness of divine grace [the worshiping people] bear in mind the needs of one another, as well as those of the whole world; and humbly wishing each human soul the highest good, they approach the divine Throne in supplication, prayer and intercession. With nothing but blessing for mankind in their hearts, the people are thus fitly preparing themselves for a right approach to the Altar. (*Agende*: xv.)

---

21 Löhe writes, "It is the most exalted practice of love where prayer is offered with one another, for one another, and for the whole world" (Schober: 77). And again, "The greatest union of souls on earth is in common prayer, in the Liturgy, the offering of the spiritual community sacrifice" (Schober: 78).

- *The Preface and Sanctus.* The Preface and the *Sanctus* are the final approach—with thanksgiving—to the foothills of the second and greater pinnacle: the New Testament Sinai. In the singing of the *Sanctus*, in anticipation of the *Verba*, the congregation has come as near to heaven as they are able in this life.

   From supplication, prayer and intercession the congregation now goes with thanksgiving on to the Preface... But the giving of thanks is soon lost in the loftier strains of the Sanctus, in the Trisagion of the heavenly hosts. In the Sanctus the worshiping people see the Lord's approach to the Sacrament, and they hail Him in prayerful Hosanna. The people can rise no higher; they are as near Heaven as it is possible for a human soul to come on earth. (*Agende*: xv.)

- *The Verba, Agnus Dei and Pater Noster.* After "a brief, but deep and expectant silence," the *Verba* brings with it the coming of Christ as the Lamb who was slain, who is now present in bread and wine with His true Body and Blood. The immediate, humble response of the congregation is again a supplication for all the needs of time and eternity, now voiced in the *Agnus Dei* and the Lord's Prayer.[22]

   Without transition the verba testamenti are now heard. He comes in the name of the Lord! God and His Lamb, slain for the sin of the world, are present! Humbled, the congregation lies before the Highest, not indeed as though cast down from the heights of the Sanctus, but by it deeply impressed with the nearness of God, commends to Him in the Agnus and Pater Noster everything which is necessary for time and eternity. (*Agende*: xv.)

- *The Pax Domini.* By the Lord's granting of His peace, He immediately calms all trembling and fear at this new and better Mt. Sinai.

---

[22] "From the most ancient times the Lord's Prayer has been placed in close union with the Consecration" (*Agende*: 42–43).

All trembling and fear, awakened anew through the coming of the Lord, now gives way to the peace of the Lord, which He Himself announces to the guests about to approach His Table. (*Agende*: xvi.)

- *The Holy Communion*. In the Holy Communion, "the worshiping congregation now receives the Sacrament of the Body and Blood of our Lord Jesus Christ." (*Agende*: xvi.) Little more can be said to encapsulate the profound simplicity of this moment. However, in connection with the distribution, a real sense of Löhe's appreciation for, and use of, both historical practice and Lutheran sensibilities can be seen in his liturgical notes on The *Confessio corporis et sanguinis Christi*:

The Confessio in the Liturgy of St. Gregory may be rendered in evangelical form somewhat as follows:—

> "The holy Body and precious Blood of our Lord Jesus Christ, the Son of God. *R*. Amen.
> "This is indeed and in truth the Body and Blood of Immanuel our God. *R*. Amen.
> I believe, I believe, I believe and will confess to my last breath that this is Thy Body which Thou tookest upon Thyself in the womb of the pure and blessed Virgin, the Mother of God, and which, out of unfeigned love, Thou gavest unto death for us. Thou hast given it for the forgiveness of our sins and for the everlasting salvation of those who receive it. This I believe to be most certainly true."

At a time, when the consciousness of confessional differences is exceedingly dull, as it appears to be at the present, and when indifference and carelessness of the word of Christ, under the guise of charity seek to implant themselves into our congregational life, it is eminently fitting to restore the Confessio corporis et sanguinis. Nevertheless in this particular caution is to be exercised for the sake of the weak; if the Confessio seems to smack of Romish processions and elevations, it may be well to omit it from the service...

We must hold with Luther, who, in a short treatise on the Sacrament, declared that the Confessio was to be reckoned among the adiaphora. It might or might not be used without sin in either case. To oppose Carlstadt and the Sacramentarians he used it, but when some of the other churches regarded it with disfavor, he also discontinued it for the sake of greater uniformity. But naturally he wished its use to be continued as expressing a confession of the Real Presence. He says:—

> "The Confessio has an excellent significance; by means of the elevation the minister in a powerful manner calls attention to the words: 'This is my body, etc.' as much as to say: 'See, dear friends, this is the body which was broken for you.' The elevation is not a symbol of sacrifice, as the Papists foolishly affirm, but an exhortation to move the people to a hearty acceptance of the doctrine of the Real Presence. In this there is not a syllable concerning sacrifice." Thus far Luther. (*Agende*: 44–45)

- *The Nunc Dimittis.* Having tasted the heavenly presence and gift of Christ, the congregation departs with enlivened hope and confidence.

This part is in the same place which it holds in the oldest liturgies of the Church... And indeed what could be more appropriate than to chant Simeon's Psalm of praise, just before leaving the sanctuary after having received the Sacrament. (*Agende*: 46)

From faith to faith, from one height to another, the devout soul has gone up to the most blessed experiences of the divine nearness and pardon. The soul can reach no higher station, except in death. The service closes, and the worshipers, with hope, born anew, seek in their daily occupations that which God has given to each as the discipline preparatory to glorification. (*Agende*: xvi.)

Proper Use of Liturgical Forms and Freedom

Obviously, Löhe sees no need to abandon the historic forms of liturgy. So long as the people are instructed in the proper understanding and use of externals, the liturgy—precisely as an *adiaphoron*—may be used *freely* as a salutary teacher of the faith and as an appropriate adornment of the Church. Indeed, as the most exquisite even of earthly existence, the liturgical worship of the Church's Divine Service should be adorned with as much beauty as possible, in order to emulate the heavenly reality at work.

If only [the] protest [against an *ex opere operato* understanding of the liturgy] were made often and solemnly, it would not be necessary to let the Church go about wearing beggar's rags. Then its prayers, its hymns, its holy ordinances, the holy thoughts of its liturgy would be impressed upon the people without their noticing it and all these things would be used as a living book for proof and instruction in sermons and catechization. (3B: 178–179)

Divine Service is the most beautiful bloom of all temporal life. The articulation and illustration of this marvelous existence should be the unity and the harmony of a worship Agenda; an aesthetic of the Church of God—not an abstract image but a concrete projection. (Löhe, *Prayer*)

Löhe is often at pains to defend himself against frequent accusations of "Romanism."[23] In response to such accusations, he often points out the abusive practices of Rome; at the same time he defends his own customs by demonstrating their decisive differences from the

---

23 "Many suspected Löhe of tending toward Romanism. A kneeling congregation at prayer during the week, singing psalms in daily services, individual confession practiced by many, issuing a Saints–calendar and a Martyr–book by Löhe — all of that together was looked upon by some with suspicion and as being Roman–like" (Schober: 81).

Romish forms. Above all else, Löhe supports his case on the basis of Scripture and with the example of the historic Lutheran Orders.

The Lutheran liturgy is a purifying and renewing of the Roman liturgy, and certainly not a destruction or even a re–building; that which is valuable and salutary has been preserved.

> The Lutheran Liturgy is an outgrowth from the Roman. The Lutheran Church itself is not a new building, but the old, cleansed from unauthorized additions. For more than three centuries the Church has advanced no new doctrines, but on the contrary has been purifying the old systems from added perversions. In a liturgical way, likewise, no new path has been marked out; but after the removal of inexpedient innovations, that which has proved valuable from the beginning has been preserved. (*Agende*: ix.)

Precisely for this reason, in those places where the Lutheran liturgy is similar to the Roman, it is not the case that the Lutherans have been "Romanizing"; rather, the Romans have in those places risen above their abuses to the higher level of *true Catholicism*.

> The Romish Church had a tendency to catholicize in those parts of the Liturgy which it holds in common with us, because in those parts the Romish Church stands high above its own standard, and agrees with that which is truly universal...
>
> To show my meaning, I point to the Romish Liturgies. They are perverted in the extreme, but in the midst of the "wood, hay and stubble," the remains of better times and of a truly Christian consciousness are to be found. Some of the old prayers cannot be changed, whether in form or substance, and will always remain adequate as expressions of the devotion of the people of God. In retaining their use, it can truly be said that the Romish Church has a catholicizing tendency; and to free them from the rubbish found in other parts of the Roman missal is an undertaking worthy of the Lutheran liturgist. (*Agende*: ix., x.–xi.)

In this way, Löhe defends and upholds the forms of worship

preserved in the Lutheran Church as a rich heritage of liturgy and hymnody. These forms are tried and true, having served in the past as a sung confession of the pure doctrine of the Lutheran Church. What is yet needed is the proper understanding of these forms, in order once again to use them appropriately.

[The performance of the liturgy as a pure confession of faith] was clearly seen at the time of the Reformation. That is why the traditional, ancient, beautiful forms were not abolished but only cleansed from sin and perversions. There are a great number of Lutheran liturgies which unite variety and simplicity. To them are added the glorious number of beautiful, matchless hymns which for three hundred years have been sung to the honor and glory of God. Our Church has a great supply of liturgical riches in its storehouses, the only thing it lacks is a proper use of them. (3B: 177)[24]

As Löhe has already indicated, the liturgy has no value *ex opere operato*; the liturgy is rather a fruit of faith and a *habitus* that must be learned, much like the catechism.

A habit must be developed again, and what has become unnatural must become natural through practice. Let us not be afraid to begin! Let him who wants to take pleasure in the services of the Lord make haste so that he may experience this joy before he departs from this world! It is true that the liturgy is a fruit of the inner life, but like the sweet fruit of a good tree it can also serve as a food which makes one desire more. Let us not be afraid to teach the liturgy! It is taught like the catechism; it can become mere lip service, just as the catechism can, but it does not need to be. We can take care that it does not; we shall not force people who cannot be taught

---

24 The proper use of the liturgy "is what the Church lacked in the days of its deepest disgrace," i.e. in the days of Rationalism following the so–called Enlightenment, "a disgrace which is today coming to an end. When its children lost their faith they also lost prayer and hymns, ornaments and beauty in their services, and now it is no easy task for the mother to bring the old children back to the old faith and the young children back to the confession of their forefathers, to bring all of them together back to the innocent and childlike way of singing and praying to God with joy" (3B: 177–178).

to learn it. (3B: 178)

Not only must the liturgy be taught and learned, however; it also serves in cooperation with formal catechesis to be itself another *teacher* of the faith. Finally, when utilized properly, the liturgy is above all else a confession of the faith; it gives voice to the heartfelt devotion of the people of God. As a *confession*, it is also a witness to those who are still learning and to those who are as yet outside the faith.

> When the liturgy is performed by devout souls it also speaks powerfully to those who are less devout, and the pure confession has no lovelier or more attractive form than when it is seen in the act of prayer and praise... The true faith is expressed not only in the sermon but is also prayed in the prayers and sung in the hymns. In this way the liturgy will serve the Church as a new defense against its enemies. It will become a holy weapon of defense and offense in the Lord's battles. (3B: 177,179)

Elsewhere, Löhe indicates that the best and most effective means of countering the ravages of the Enlightenment would be the consistent practice of churchly worship and corporate, liturgical prayer.

> If a genuine, orderly, uniting of souls in the exalted activity of worship existed in our Church; or if freedom were given to establish such a union where appreciation and ability were present, then the most holy practice and the most holy life of our fellowship would be transferred to where it belongs—the House of God. The cause would have its most beautiful climax and would have found the best way also, of reaching little by little those church members who are still serving the world. (Schober: 78)

Löhe comprehends well the Lutheran understanding of worship as *Gottesdienst*, a Divine Service in which the service of God to man has priority over the service of man to God. The Lord first speaks His Word to His people, calls and gathers them by His Gospel, and showers them with His heavenly gifts; His people respond by speaking "as the oracles of God" (1 Peter 4:11), confessing to Him (as the highest act of worship) all that He has said and done for man.

It is the foundational character of this *Gottesdienst*, this divine–earthly conversation, that finally determines the shape of the liturgy. As already explained by Löhe in his commentary on the Divine Service, the dual poles of Word and Sacrament provide the unmovable points of reference for the Church's approach to God. Through these means, God speaks to His people; by the use of these same means, His people lay hold of Him by faith and speak to Him in response.[25] This beautiful dialogue between God and man, in which God retains at all times the initiative, is for Löhe the essence of liturgical worship. The liturgy embodies the dialogue, while the Holy Spirit guides the Church in her response to the holy conversation of God.

> [The Church] worships as it speaks and as it sings, and the Lord dwells among its songs of praise with His Sacraments. Its approach to him, his approach to it—these holy forms of its approach and His coming we call the liturgy... Just as the stars revolve around the sun, so does the congregation in its services, full of loveliness and dignity, revolve around its Lord. In holy, childlike innocence which only a child's innocent heart understands properly, the multitude of redeemed, sanctified children of God dances in worship around the universal Father and the Lamb, and the Spirit of the Lord of lords guides their steps. The spiritual joy and heavenly delight enjoyed by those who take part in this sort of liturgy cannot be described. (3B: 176–177)

---

25 By way of example, Löhe describes the Lord's Supper in his Catechism as not only our remembrance of Christ, but especially as His "remembrance" of us in the giving of His Body and His Blood. In response to the catechetical question, *Do we commemorate Him only?*, Löhe gives the answer:

> No, He remembers us and our need much more, and in the Bread gives to us His Body for the remission of sins. We remember Him in receiving the bread, and He remembers us by giving us in, with and under the bread His Body, that we may become members of His Body, His flesh and blood; and He gives to us forgiveness of sins, that body and soul may rejoice in the Living God. (Löhe, *Questions and Answers*: 173)

In this way, the Divine Service becomes the occasion for the Church on earth to experience the nearness of her heavenly Bridegroom more fully than anywhere else in this life.

Löhe's Liturgical Theology in Practice:

Regardless of what he was doing, Wilhelm Löhe always saw himself above all else a *pastor*; "a spiritual counselor, a curate of souls—all that is implied in the German word *Seelsorger*." (Heintzen–1964: 23) And as a *Seelsorger*, Löhe had a profound influence over his people. Apparently, even in cases solely physical in nature, the people put more confidence in Löhe as their "eternal helper" than in their "earthly doctor." Whether this was altogether good is debatable, but it surely had much to do with Löhe's approach to pastoral ministry and care. He consciously "exercised mildness, sympathy and a concern for the tiniest need of his people." (Greenholt: 4–5) He had profound insight into the psychological state of his members, and "as a counselor he was instrumental in helping troubled individuals find assurance and peace." One example is Lorenz Loesel, "a young peasant, who later became the first volunteer for Löhe's missionary colony in America. As the result of a troubled conscience, Loesel had been depressed for two months, during which he would neither talk nor work. Löhe attended him daily for several weeks and was able to report that Loesel had recovered." (Heintzen–1964: 24) But despite his sensitivity to the physical and psychological hurts of his members, Löhe did not pretend to be a doctor. "He sometimes gave medical advice in his younger years; but he soon abandoned this, warned fellow clergymen against it, and advised his parishioners to obtain the services of physicians." (Ottersberg: 181) Nor did Löhe try to play the "junior psychiatrist." In every respect of his ministry, the Word of God was central, and he clearly approached his cure of souls as a *spiritual cure*. Referring specifically to the Lutheran Church, but surely also as a projection of his own attitude, Löhe writes:

> [The Lutheran Church] does not consider it an insult, nor is it eager to interpret it as an insult, when someone says, "This pastor thinks it is enough if he preaches, catechizes, administers the sacraments, hears confessions, and comforts the

sick!" It knows that even the most faithful pastors do not do enough of this. It has little use for multiplying pastoral duties but treasures those which are commanded in the Scriptures and have been recognized since ancient times. To many people it is something novel that a man should not be a jack of many trades but a master of the few precious means, yet this is what the church has always thought. In a word, it accomplishes much through a few means. (3B: 165)[26]

He then goes on to write that "preaching, sacrament, catechization, and also the liturgy take care of souls in a truly magnificent way. The care of individual souls is dependent on the rapport that results from sermon, sacrament, and catechization." (3B: 174) As a description of Löhe's approach to pastoral ministry, these remarks accurately reflect, as well, his understanding and practice of liturgical theology; it could even be said that his pastoral ministry is in many ways simply the incarnation of his liturgical theology.

Löhe's liturgical theology and pastoral practice came together most closely in the Lord's Supper; indeed, his entire ministry centered around the Sacrament of the Altar. Here at the Altar, he found not only the very heart of his own faith, but the heartbeat of the Church and of his congregation, as well. For him, the Christian life was a continuous "change between receiving the eucharist and preparation for it." Everything that Löhe did—as pastor and as liturgiologist—as well as all that he desired for the parish, can therefore be understood only on the basis of the Lord's most holy Altar. (Schober: 54–55) As Löhe writes: "All our performance, be it little or much, has in the past had no other intention and has no other now, than to honor the creative words of our most holy Consecrator in the Sacrament of the Altar. We poor people of Dettelsau desire to dedicate all our entire work as a trifling but ever–blooming wreath of gratitude and praise to His Altar." (Schober: 55)

Löhe's emphasis on the Eucharist was by no means to the exclusion of the Word of God as proclaimed in such other forms as

---

26 Toward the end of his ministry, Löhe put his theology of pastoral care into a textbook for ministerial students. "*Der evangelische Geistliche*, in *Werke*, III/2, 7–317, was published as two volumes in 1853 and 1858" (3B: 17n57).

Scripture, preaching, and Baptism. The means of grace, as God's gracious and forgiving Word—the "bright and clear Center of the Church" (3B: 64)—"are the source and gathering point of the visible as also the invisible Church." (Schober: 50) For Löhe, as for the Lutheran Church in her Confessions, "the Lord gives his Holy Spirit only through His Word and Sacraments." (3B: 164) He writes:

> The word calls from the world to the Church, Baptism unites those who are called by the word into the body of Christ and fills them with the Holy Spirit, the eucharist nourishes the branches on the vine—the members of Christ—that they remain branches and members and produce much fruit... Without a doubt, they are of the greatest significance for the body of Christ; not simply church orders, but firm laws of God and at the same time gifts of grace; yea, the hand of God with which he builds the eternal temple of the body of Christ. (Schober: 50)

Just as he had come to see the Lord's Supper as the primary point of disagreement between the Lutherans and Reformed, so Löhe also understood the means of grace as the source of the Church's identity.

> What distinguishes the Church from all other groups in the world is its possession of the pure Word and Sacraments, and that which distinguishes each denomination from all others is the way it understands the Word and administers the Sacraments... As the Church would cease to be the Church if it no longer had God's Word and Sacraments, so the denomination would cease to be what it is if it would lose its peculiar understanding of the Word and its peculiar use of the Sacraments. (3B: 106)

How highly Löhe regarded Baptism, in particular, and the extent to which he incorporated this Sacrament also into his ministry, is shown for example in his publication of a collection of Luther's writings on Baptism. He writes in the introduction to this work: "Let us frequently admonish the parents to remind the children of the great blessings of their Baptism; it is shameful that Baptism is so largely forgotten, especially since it offers an abundance of doctrine, comfort...and justice." (Schober: 53–54)

Löhe's firm conviction about the Word and Sacraments is no doubt also the reason for his pastoral and liturgical integrity. For if the Church has Her identity only in the means of grace, then there is no reason or excuse for experimenting with new and different means or methods of ministry. But while Löhe did not introduce any new means of pastoral care, he did *reintroduce* the much neglected means of Confession and Absolution.

> Men overlooked what is central in pastoral care: the confessional. Since private confession and the examination and absolution connected with it were no longer practiced, the pastor could find neither a dignified, quiet, secluded, unsuspected place for carrying out his care of souls nor a detached, holy relationship to the penitent. Just because of this the right frame of mind was lacking for the pastor as well as for the penitent seeking advice. They were almost embarrassed as they tried, the one to apply God's Word to only one person and the other to accept the pastor's word as God's Word to only *one* soul... There was never a greater sin against the care of souls than when unjustified... objections... were used as the reason for taking away from the pastor his right to examine and for taking away from the penitent the benefit of private confession and absolution. All other methods of individual care of souls have proved unsatisfactory and often impracticable substitutes for private confession. (3B: 174–175)

In the context of Löhe's liturgical theology, Confession and Absolution stands on the edge between "ordinary" and "extraordinary" pastoral care. It is *extraordinary* because it is a means of pastoral care to the individual; and yet, it is the *ordinary* means whereby the individual is regularly reincorporated into the worshipping body.[27] For Löhe, the liturgical worship of the Church is the ordinary and most proper place for pastoral care to occur; consider again his understand-

[27] cf. Korby, *The Theology of Pastoral Care in Wilhelm Löhe*, for a thorough explanation of Löhe's understanding and use of *ordinary* and *extraordinary* pastoral care. We note here that "Löhe reckoned the liturgy among the ordinary means for the care of souls" (Korby: 273).

ing of the Christian life as a continuous movement to and from the Altar of Christ. Thus, even the liturgy of individual Confession and Absolution is enacted with a view to the corporate liturgical action.[28]

When Löhe first arrived in Neuendettelsau, the practice of Private Confession was virtually unheard of, though the service of public confession was being used. He strongly believed in the benefits of a personal Absolution, and considered it the church's duty to provide this opportunity. As he writes:

> Private Confession is for the individual commanded neither by God nor the Church, but it is a permission and a blessed privilege... The Church sees to it that by means of instruction and exhortation this glorious opportunity for furtherance of the spiritual life not be neglected, but at all times be searched for and used so that the blessing residing in it be accepted with joy and thanksgiving. (Schober: 70)

Still, Löhe did not act with undue haste in the Neuendettelsau parish. In fact, "for several years Löhe confined himself to the use of common confession," but all the while "continued to stress the blessing of private confession in instruction and in his addresses." (Ottersberg: 180) Apparently, a few of the parishioners eventually requested that Löhe hear their individual confessions and grant them personal Absolution. And when he announced the opportunity for such Private Confession and Absolution following a service of public confession, "he was amazed to find the entire congregation waiting to see him individually in the sacristy." Henceforth, though he always continued the practice of public confessional services, most of the members preferred to come to Pastor Löhe privately for Absolution. (3B: 16–17) Pastor Bezzel, Löhe's successor at Neuendettelsau, comments:

> Löhe knew human nature well, and was able to judge in a masterful way the condition of the soul in the presence of

---

[28] For an excellent treatment of Confession in the context of Löhe's liturgical theology, especially as it relates to the Lord's Supper, cf. Schattauer, *Announcement, Confession, and Lord's Supper in the Pastoral–Liturgical Work of Wilhelm Löhe*. This masterful work examines not only Löhe's theory but also his actual practice of liturgical theology in the Neuendettelsau parish.

certain symptoms with the help of the Word of God... The private, individual, Confession in which he spoke that word... not as a new arrangement but as a richly blessed practice... [was] used without force, in pastoral modesty, in priestly patience, not as torture for the conscience, but as a comfort for the distressed soul... He knew how to observe the word of the old Father: "Do not be ashamed to confess your sin, for you do not know whether I have not committed the same or even greater ones." (Schober: 63–64)

As to the form of a private confession, Löhe enumerates five possibilities:

(a.) The personal exhortation without the enumeration of special sins. In this situation an established fixed method of procedure is enough.
(b.) Forgiveness is desired for a certain length of time, as a rule the period of time being between one Communion and the next, or for special sins. In this case the sins must be named.
(c.) A third aim is to get advice in behalf of avoiding new sins; to receive remedies against certain sinful conditions and temptations. In this case a confessional conversation, which has the same merit as the free private confession is suitable.
(d.) There is also a detailed private confession in which the confessing person wishes to give the pastor a more intimate knowledge of himself. This type of confession develops into a biography and had best be done in writing. In this case the pastor has to have time to read and think about it.
(e.) Finally, a Christian can in his confession have the purpose to humble himself, even if he knows and believes that his sins are forgiven him. Therewith he desires to kill the old nature and suppress thoroughly his self–righteousness. This type of private confession is the most rare, but it is a very exalted one. (Schober: 70)

Aside from the particular form of an individual confession, Löhe highlights four essential component parts; namely, that the penitent say in some manner:

(1.) I am a sinner.
(2.) I believe in forgiveness of sin through Jesus Christ.
(3.) I beg for absolution.
(4.) I do want to mend my ways. (Schober: 71)

Even such a simple private confession as this, Löhe maintains, "is always preferable to the common confession" (Schober: 71).[29]

LÖHE'S MISSIONARY EFFORTS IN AMERICA...

...Among the German Lutherans:

As already indicated, Pastor Wilhelm Löhe's missionary efforts extended far beyond the borders of his Neuendettelsau parish. Chief among such efforts were his contributions to the Lutheran Church in North America.

The catalyst that triggered Löhe's activity on behalf of the German Lutherans in America was a plea for help from Pastor Friedrich Conrad Dietrich Wyneken. A German emigrant who had come to America as a missionary, Wyneken was the pastor of congregations at Friedheim and Fort Wayne, Indiana, and a missionary on horseback to northwestern Ohio, southern Michigan and northern Indiana. (cf. Heintzen–1973: 15) He saw the difficult situation of so many of his fellow Germans in America and was especially concerned for their spiritual welfare. "The scarcity of pastors was recognized as the main danger confronting the Lutheran Church in America. In 1840 there were 400 pastors to care for 120,000 communicant members, grouped in 1200 congregations." (Schaaf–1961: 5) Wyneken saw the need and put forth "the Macedonian call, 'Come over and help us.'" (Schaaf–1961: 7) One of his moving pleas for help reads in part:

> Material conditions improve, want is relieved, the fields flourish, the log huts have disappeared and made room for statlier

---
[29] For additional information, cf. Wittenberg, "Wilhelm Löhe and Confession." This wonderful little essay describes the manner in which Pastor Löhe incorporated Private Confession and Absolution into the life of his parish. It includes some touching observations from the diary of a young girl who benefited from Löhe's pastoral care.

homes, you see better clothing and more cheerful faces. But look at their souls—for years they have been without the Word of life, no Table of the Lord has been spread for them. They have grown used to their spiritual death... Now, behold the young and old are lying on their deathbeds... The poor soul stares into solemn eternity, the shudders of death dim the vision of the spirit, so that it cannot behold the reconciled God and Mediator, the merciful High Priest in the holy of Holies. Oh, what a blessing the ambassador of peace would now be! (Heintzen–1964: 41–42)

It is easy to see how such appeals would move the pastoral heart of a man like Wilhelm Löhe. Wyneken wrote long letters to Pastor Schmidt of Pittsburgh, who in turn published them in his newspaper, the *Lutheran Church News*. This newspaper circulated among Lutherans in Europe, where it was "frequently excerpted and reprinted in still other publications in Germany" (Heintzen–1973: 16). One of these "other publications" that included quotes from Wyneken's articles was a pamphlet entitled *Aufruf zur Unterstuetzung der Deutsch–Protestantischen Kirche in Nordamerika* (*Summons for the Support of the German–Protestant Church in North America*), issued in 1840 by the founders of a missionary society in Stade, Hanover. It was this Stade "Summons" that Löhe read on a visit to Erlangen and that moved him to act. (cf. Heintzen–1964: 42–43)

The first thing Löhe did in response to the Stade "Summons" was to write an article of his own, "The Lutheran Emigrants in North America: An Address to the Readers." This he had published in the Noerdlingen *Sonntagsblatt*, a weekly newspaper circulated in Franconia and edited by his close friend, Pastor John Frederick Wucherer. (cf. 3B: 18) Following Wyneken's example, Löhe's article portrayed the spiritual poverty of the German Lutherans in North America. He pointed out that these were fellow Germans, and perhaps even close relatives, who were in such desperate need. And he noted that without pastoral care they were falling prey to the Romanists and Methodists. (cf. Heintzen–1964: 45) Löhe writes:

Our brethren are living in the wilderness of North America without nourishment for their souls! We are sitting on our hands and are forgetting to help them! All the more eagerly do the servants of the pope and the lovers of sects approach them. Their love also appears holy; sufferers do not reject them. They return the love and with their children turn to the Roman church and the sects! To [the] thirsty [even] muddy, unclean, unhealthy water is preferable to dying of thirst. And we should not give them help? We should behold how our brethren in the faith are being misled because of lack of shepherds. (Schober: 89–90)

Above all, Löhe exposed the gross hypocrisy of talking about, praying for, and supporting heathen missions, while letting fellow Christians spiritually starve to death.

Shame on us if we here do not do what we can! Will we support our church's missions among the heathen, yet let already established congregations go under? Shall we let thousands starve while we devote so much attention to win individuals? We pray that the Lord will gather one holy Church among the heathen, and are we then to let established congregations fall prey to this temptation [of the Romanists and various sects]? We forget those who are so near to us while we stretch out to those who still serve idols. We should not do one and forget the other! Up, brethren, let us help as much as we are able! (3B: 18–19)

Then, quoting from the Stade "Summons," Löhe urged: "I beseech you for the sake of Christ, put your hand to the work, unite for immediate action! Don't spend time deliberating. Hurry, hurry! The main thing is to save immortal souls!" (Heintzen–1964: 45)

With such exhortations, Löhe included specific directives, not leaving his readers in the dark as to what they should be doing:

If there is someone among you who can go, a pastor, a ministerial candidate, who is not bound by other duties, a young school teacher or someone who is suited to teaching: over there is work. There you can dispense the riches of the Gospel you have gathered, and the Lord will fill you anew with His good gifts. If there is someone who cannot go...he can by means of liberal donations make it possible for others to go... Should a faithful pastor of a local church read this, let him show his congregation how to help. Let everyone do what he can! All of us want to pray in the church, at home, at morning and evening, that the Lord will not forsake the forsaken and that He will lead the straying sheep home. (Heintzen–1964: 46)

With respect to Löhe's written appeals for help, it should also be noted that,
> [He] assisted Wyneken in writing and publishing his celebrated pamphlet, *The Distress of the German Lutherans in North America* [when Wyneken visited Neuendettelsau in the late spring of 1842]. Under five headings this tract graphically depicted: the spiritual destitution of the majority of German Lutheran immigrants, the dangers they faced from sects and Romanists, the inner decay through religious unionism and "new measurism," the dark outlook for the future, and the means to help. (Heintzen–1964: 65)

Besides the initial article in the *Sonntagsblatt*, Löhe and Wucherer also collaborated in founding an important missionary periodical, *Kirchliche Mittheilungen aus und ueber Nord–Amerika* (*Church News From and About North America*). The first issue appeared in March 1843 and was four pages long. The first run of the periodical, a distribution of 8,000 copies, provided a profit of 2,000 gulden for the mission to North America. And the subscription list four years later still numbered over 5,000. The *Kirchliche Mittheilungen* was especially significant for the "German missionary enterprise," in that "it served as a clearing–house for the various working groups; it aroused and maintained keen interest in the movement, produced needed funds, recruited new workers, and provided the unifying agency needed by this volunteer, loose–jointed, missionary arm." (Heintzen–1964: 68–69)

Now, to back up again, the response to Löhe's initial article in the *Sonntagsblatt* included the donation of 600 gulden for support of the mission to North America. (cf. Schober: 90) At first, there were no volunteers who could actually be sent, but eventually two were found: "Adam Ernst, a young shoemaker who had once been Pastor Wucherer's parishioner," and "George Burger, a weaver from Wucherer's present congregation." Neither of the men was the "pastor, ministerial candidate, or school teacher" hoped for, but Löhe agreed to train them as school–teachers for the American frontier. So Löhe's home became a seminary of sorts, in which he established "a one–year crash course that one graduate later referred to as 'the Neuendettelsau purgatory.'" (Heintzen–1973: 18) This "seminary" in Löhe's home was "the foundation for the later '*Missions and Diasporaseminar*' (Missions and Diaspora Seminary) of Neuendettelsau which for years carried the inscription '*Missionsanstalt fuer Nordamerika*' (Missionary Institution for North America)." (Schober: 91)

The training and education Löhe gave his *Nothhelfer* (i.e. "emergency men") was abbreviated and brisk to be sure, but also surprisingly broad in its scope. For instance, in less than a year, primarily during the winter of 1841/42, Löhe taught Ernst and Burger: German grammar, English, writing, and penmanship; Christian doctrine, Lutheran symbolics, Bible history, and Church history; geography, American history, and the beliefs of various American denominations; pastoral theology, catechetics, homiletics, liturgics, and ethics. The two men gained practical experience as they "delivered short addresses at vesper services; catechised children under Löhe's supervision; and accompanied him on the visits to the sick." (Greenholt: 38; also, cf. Heintzen–1964: 48; and Schaaf–1961: 19) "They were required to instruct a blind boy and make numerous visits to the sick and dying in Neuendettelsau. In order that the two could learn music, an old piano was bought for 3 fl., and singing and piano playing were taught by a friend of Löhe's from Windsbach." All of this, and yet already by the spring of 1842 Löhe felt the men were ready to be sent as emergency helpers to the German Lutherans of North America. (Schaaf–1961: 19–20) They were being sent primarily as school–teachers and were to enter the Office of the Holy Ministry only if they came "into a region where children need Baptism and confirmation, the confirmed Absolution and the Sacrament of the Altar and betrothed people marriage"; and only then by offering themselves for ordination to an evangelical Lutheran synod or ministerium committed to the Lutheran Confessions. (Greenholt: 39) All of this and more was explained in a document of instructions for the two missionaries, typical of the kind Löhe would continue to provide for each of the many men he sent to America in later years (e.g., cf. MF: 98–101). Both Löhe and Wucherer signed these documents of instruction and thereby took responsibility for the missionary effort centered out of Neuendettelsau. (cf. Schaaf–1961: 20–21) "Over the course of years more than three hundred men were sent from the missionary seminary in Neuendettelsau to North America. The last two men went out in 1925." (3B: 21n68)

There were criticisms levelled at Löhe for allowing his *Nothhelfer* to enter the ministry in America without the usual, far more thorough education. But Löhe's response was that, while he recognized the preference for and the advantage of an educated clergy, he believed the men he sent to be the best available and that the dire need for pastors in America required action. (cf. Greenholt: 48)

> If one were to wait till the emigrant Germans could be provided with preachers prepared in the German fashion, perhaps many decades would meanwhile elapse, many hundreds of children would be unbaptized, and many adults would be uninstructed, unconfirmed, unabsolved, without the Sacrament of the Altar, and besides that, would die in concubinage and adultery. *Need has no law*. It is always awkward when midwives must undertake emergency Baptisms, but still it is better for children to be baptized by midwives than not at all. Everyone understands that. In this way one must regard also the appointment of scantily-educated preachers in America. They are emergency helpers (*Nothhelfer*); they should be nothing else and want to be nothing else. (MF: 98)

Thus, as one biographer describes:

> Where necessary the pastor served both as minister and school–teacher. His outstanding virtues were to be wisdom and humility, simplicity and dignity. As preacher he was obligated to preach the "pure word" of God. Löhe deplored the susceptibility of America to the "gift of gab." In choosing *Nothhelfer* he was not primarily concerned with the abil-

ity to preach, since administering the Sacraments, teaching children, and conducting the liturgy were just as important as preaching. And the non–talkative were qualified to do these. (Greenholt: 51)

Clearly, Löhe's high valuation of the means of grace prompted him to be flexible in meeting the need of the German Lutherans in North America. Even so, Löhe did not oppose additional training for the *Nothhelfer* in America, but rather encouraged it. (cf. Greenholt: 49)

As to the question of a proper call and ordination for the *Nothhelfer*, Löhe felt quite strongly that the men must be *rite vocati*, according to the *Augustana*, Article XIV. But he also believed that the general cry for help from the German Lutherans in America was truly a genuine call that could rightly be extended by committee to qualified candidates in Germany. The ordination, on the other hand, he felt should more properly be left to an appropriate American synod. (cf. Schaaf–1961: 28) In any case, Löhe held that "ordination was of less importance than the 'call' because one could, if rightly called, enter the ministry without ordination, the latter being merely the 'public testimony of the call.'" (Greenholt: 51)

As an interesting side note, though Löhe discouraged foreign missionaries from "towing" wives along with them, he did not oppose the marriage of settled mission–pastors. In fact, he was informed at one point—and apparently agreed—that "two things were indispensable for a missionary preacher in the 'bush': a horse because he must go to others; a wife because he must live apart from others." (Greenholt: 52)

Returning to the two original *Nothhelfer*, soon after their arrival in America, Ernst and Burger became associated with the Ohio Synod. Burger, who was unable to find work either as a school–teacher or as a weaver, enrolled in the Synod's seminary in Columbus, Ohio. Ernst began a school nearby. Eventually both men became pastors of the Ohio Synod. While still a student at the seminary, Burger so impressed his teachers with his zeal for the ministry that they contacted Pastor Löhe, "commending the emergency men and urging the Neuendettelsau pastor to send more like them." (Heintzen–1973: 20) Thus began the relationship between the Ohio Synod and Wilhelm Löhe. And when he was assured of the synod's loyalty to the Lutheran

Confessions, Löhe responded to their requests with sympathy and generosity. (cf. Heintzen–1964: 57–58) An excerpt from one of the Ohio Synod's pleas for help reads:

> We need more students and we need support for many who apply; they are for the most part poor who wish to dedicate themselves to the preaching of the Word of God. Oh, that friends and brethren in the Fatherland would mightily espouse the cause of the Church here [in America], and every year send us a number of previously trained young men of the caliber of Ernst and Burger!... Further, what we need, desperately need, is books of the right sort. The seminary has barely made a beginning of a library. Brethren... who are not able to assist us in other ways, can help in this way! Is not Germany the land of all literature? How can our church here [in America] guard her purity if her preachers do not know German literature? (Heintzen–1964: 58)

Löhe's response included the provision of each of these; namely, more men, money and books. "Books began to be sent immediately. Funds were shared. And gradually more and more men were channeled through Pastor Löhe to help the brethren on the American frontier." (Heintzen–1973: 21)

Cooperation between Löhe and the Ohio Synod waned, however, as the movement known as "American Lutheranism" began to erode the confessional integrity of the synod.

"American Lutheranism" was a movement, led primarily by men who had been in America all their lives, which wanted to divest the Lutheran Church of its foreign heritage and give it a character more appropriate for the American scene. It advocated the adoption of practices common to other American Protestant groups, such as revivals and other methods grouped together under the general heading of "new measures." It also proposed modifying the Augsburg Confession to adapt it to the American scene. (3B: 21n69)

Evidence for the intrusion of "new measures" into the Ohio Synod was most obvious in the switch from German to English in the classrooms of the seminary. At that point, Löhe directed his *Nothhelfer* to seek new associations with "men more kindly disposed to a strong confessional stance and to the retention of the German language and religion." Specifically in mind was a group of German Lutherans from Saxony who had settled in Missouri. Thus, in September 1845, a total of 15 men sent by Wilhelm Löhe met in Cleveland with representatives of the Missouri Lutherans, to lay the foundation for a truly *confessional* Lutheran Synod. "From this meeting came the organization of the Missouri Synod in Fort Wayne, Indiana, the following July." Obviously, from that point on, Löhe could no longer use the Ohio Synod's seminary as a channel for his *Nothhelfer*, so the Neuendettelsau pastor took steps to establish a new seminary in Fort Wayne, Indiana to continue providing pastors for the German Lutherans in North America. (3B: 21–22)

> In view of the great need here and to avoid future shortage [Löhe and other faithful Lutheran friends in Germany] have formulated the plan to establish a seminary in Fort Wayne. There believing young men, who have been endowed with the necessary talents, can be trained for future participation in the office of the holy ministry in the Lutheran Church. (MF: 216)

Löhe intended the Fort Wayne seminary to be very "practical" in nature, for the training of pastors as quickly as possible. (cf. Heintzen–1964: 163) He immediately provided "a candidate of theology [K. A. W. Roebbelen] and 11 young men who for a shorter or longer period of time had received instruction already in Germany from tested Lutheran pastors." (MF: 216) And as before in Ohio, Löhe would continue to send students to the new Fort Wayne seminary in years ahead.

> [The seminary at first] was quartered in a rented building, but funds from Germany made possible the purchase of land which might later serve as campus and the rent from which was available for expenses. Löhe also assumed responsibility for salaries and furnished theological books. The students then in preparation in Germany entered the new American seminary, and a preparatory institution was opened [in Nuremberg]...to serve as a feeder. (Ottersberg: 186)

Recognizing the significance of the new seminary, the Missouri Synod in 1847 at its first convention requested that Pastor Löhe transfer ownership of the school to the synod and within a few months Löhe honored their request. Yet, because the young synod was unable to support the seminary by itself and had therefore also asked Löhe to continue his support, he pledged to provide for the school "as far as our limited powers permit and as God grants us the means." (Heintzen–1973: 48–49) Pastor Löhe did, however, lay down conditions with his gift. He and Pastor Wucherer stipulated:

(1.) that [the seminary] serve the Lutheran Church for all time and train pastors and shepherds for it only;

(2.) that the German language be and remain inviolably the only medium of instruction;

(3.) that the seminary remain what it is: namely, an institution for the training, as quickly and thoroughly as possible, of preachers and pastors for the innumerable orphaned German fellow believers and the newly–immigrated congregations of our race and confession. It should not be a theological institution in the usual sense of the word, but a nursery of preachers and pastors whose study would be a serious preparation for the holy office itself. (Heintzen–1973: 48)

Among his many contributions to the infant Missouri Synod, the Fort Wayne seminary stands out as one of Löhe's most important gifts. It is an embodiment of his burning zeal for missions and a prominent example of his selfless support of his American brothers in Christ. Chiefly by way of the seminary, Löhe provided some 82 pastors for the Missouri Synod during the years he was associated with it. (cf. Heintzen–1964: 78) Accordingly, a simple but probably accurate assessment of the early Missouri Synod regards it as a blend of "Saxon 'orthodoxy' and Löhe 'activism.'" (MF: 90) As one biographer notes:

The legacy of Löhe in the Missouri Synod is preserved in its practical rather than its theological heritage. Witness his contributions of students, pastors, congregations, institutions, money, and a vital practical missionary spirit. The impact of these assets on the struggling young Synod, and its later history down to the present, is difficult to overestimate. Beyond all doubt, without Löhe's forces the beginnings and growth of the Synod would have been critically hindered. (Heintzen–1964: 248)[30]

...Among the Heathen American Indians in Michigan:

Besides the founding and support of the Fort Wayne seminary, nowhere is Löhe's *activism* more obvious than in his activity on behalf of the heathen American Indians. From the first, alongside his interest in providing pastors for the German Lutherans in America, Löhe was also interested in reaching the American Indians with the Gospel. Already in 1843, he wrote of his concern for these people in an article entitled, "*Dia Mission unter der Heiden*" (i.e. "The Mission among the Heathens"): "One should be forced through compassion to render the last service to these tribes which are disappearing from the earth by giving them the light of the Gospel to light up their path to eternity." (Schober: 91)

Early on, a friend suggested to Löhe that a special "Indian Mission Seminary" be established with the Ohio Synod's seminary in Columbus. But Löhe had other plans. His interest had been piqued by the success of Pastor Friederich Schmid of the Basel Mission, who had already been working among the Indians around Ann Arbor, Michigan. And he was thereby encouraged to establish congregations among or near the Indians, and to provide them with capable preachers who would not only shepherd their flocks but also evangelize the Indians. This approach would merge conveniently with Löhe's plans to establish congregational colonies among those Lutherans who were emigrating from Germany to North America. He strongly believed that by grouping these German Lutheran emigrants together even before they left, and by providing them with pastors to accompany them from the start, they would be far less likely to fall from the Church and from the faith after they arrived in the New World. Such colo-

---

30 For additional information, cf. Heintzen, *Wilhelm Löhe and the Missouri Synod*; also, Schaaf, *Wilhelm Löhe's Relation to the American Church*.

nies would also then provide a place for later emigrants to go. And, according to Löhe's ideas, they would serve as missionary stations from which to evangelize the American Indians. (cf. Schaaf–1961: 67–69) "'It is best,' [Löhe] wrote, `if mission work can be done out of existing congregations. Such congregations are mission colonies, which afford the missionary many advantages over being alone.'" (Heintzen–1973: 30)

Pastor Löhe wasted little time in pursuing his "colonization" plan. Already with the sending of his third *Nothhelfer*, George Wilhelm Hattstaedt, Löhe included in his document of instructions that Hattstaedt should contact the Missouri Lutherans and share with them the need for work among the American Indians. (cf. Greenholt: 57) Löhe writes,

> In particular you are to ascertain which Lutheran, specifically which German Lutheran congregations, live in the midst or in the vicinity of heathen Indian tribes. And you are to hold consultation with [the faithful emigrant Saxon pastors] concerning our desire that the same persons be both pastors and missionaries to the heathen. You are to make the most careful inquiry about missionaries of various confessions who are working among the heathen Indians, to find out what has been done for those tribes particularly by our brethren in the faith and what we can possibly do to work together with already existing Indian missions. (MF: 100–101)

Hattstaedt, in fact, did not establish any working relationship with the Missouri Lutherans, since he rather quickly became the pastor of Trinity Lutheran Church in Monroe, Michigan. Once there, he joined the Michigan Synod, founded by Friedrich Schmid in 1840. So Löhe, through his *Nothhelfer*, became acquainted "first hand" with Schmid's missionary work among the American Indians. (cf. Zehnder: 18) Since Schmid's success had already impressed him in the past, and since the Michigan Synod appeared to be a staunch confessional group, Löhe was happy to cooperate with their existing Indian missions. (cf. Greenholt: 65)

Based on reports from, and correspondence with, both Hattstaedt and Schmid, Löhe determined that the northern area of Michigan would be an ideal location for his colonization plan. And after receiving a more detailed "scouting report" from Schmid and J. J. F. Auch (the Michigan Synod's first Indian missionary), he selected a spot on the Cass River—about 15 miles from the town of Saginaw, Michigan—as the place to start. (cf. Schaaf–1961: 78) Meanwhile, Pastor Löhe was also gathering the group of German Lutherans who would make up the first of his colonies.

The first person to volunteer for Löhe's mission colony was Lorenz Loesel, a formerly-troubled young man to whom Pastor Löhe had brought spiritual peace and who had since been working for Löhe as a hostler. (cf. Zehnder: 18–19) Loesel took to the project with joyful enthusiasm and began to enlist others to accompany him on the journey to America. Before long, a small group of Franconian peasants and artisans had been gathered to form the colony. A pastor had also been found in the person of August Craemer, a ministerial candidate who had come to Neuendettelsau in the autumn of 1844. (cf. Greenholt: 67) "Craemer was fluent in the use of the English language, having been a tutor of German at Oxford, and a man with a genuine missionary spirit." (Schaaf–1961: 71) Appropriately, the little group took for the name of their colony, *Frankenmuth*, meaning "Courage of the Franconians." (cf. Heintzen–1973: 31)

The Frankenmuth colonists met with Pastor Löhe in Neuendettelsau during the winter of 1844/45, Saturday evenings and Sundays, in preparation for their journey and the founding of the missionary colony. They discussed the institution of the colony's ecclesiastical life; they studied doctrine; they practiced the liturgy and learned hymns; and they assisted Löhe in the composition of their 88–paragraph constitution: *Kirchenordnung der deutsch–lutherischen Missionsgemeinde Frankenmuth*. (cf. Greenholt: 69)[31] In all things, they were urged to practice humility and to sacrifice personal interests for the sake of the colony. (cf. Greenholt: 69) The small group decided to leave Germany for the "new world" in the spring of 1845. (cf. Zehnder: 20) Before setting sail from Bremerhaven on the 20th of April, they extended a call to Pastor Craemer and formally subscribed to the *Kirchenordnung*. And with the help of some friends of Pastor Löhe in Mecklenburg, Craemer was ordained in the Schwerin Ca-

---

31 For an English translation of the *Kirchenordnung*, cf. MF: 110–115.

thedral. (cf. Schaaf–1961: 71) About that same time, Löhe wrote to his little colony:

> My dear children whom I nurtured for a year with milk and sweet food, yes also with the food of adults, be my letter to the heathen. (Greenholt: 69)

> From your Christian way of life and your piety the heathen are to recognize how pleasant it is to have fellowship with Jesus. (Zehnder: 11)

And Löhe writes with obvious pride in his dear colonists: "No earthly necessity drove them to leave their fatherland. In the homeland, which they loved, they enjoyed a good life... It was a noble idea that moved them." (Zehnder: 21)

The colonists established *Frankenmuth* at the chosen location in the Saginaw Valley of Michigan, on 680 acres of land purchased for their little village. They began construction of cabins and a church immediately. (cf. Schaaf–1961: 73) And "from the first Frankenmuth's purpose as a religious colony was established. Every Sunday the colony gathered for liturgically correct services, conducted just as they had been in the Bavarian village churches the settlers had known. And every morning and evening of the week the group assembled for devotions." Meanwhile, Pastor Craemer began to make walking tours of the surrounding wilderness areas, to visit the Indian encampments of the Chippewa tribe. Over time, he gained the confidence of several tribal chiefs, who agreed to send their children to Frankenmuth for education and Christian instruction. Pastor Craemer also set about learning the Chippewa language and translated Luther's Small Catechism into the Chippewa tongue. By Christmas of 1846, when the colony dedicated its first church, the first three Chippewa converts were baptized. Earlier that year, Löhe had sent 90 additonal German emigrants, including seven new missionary–colonists (one of them, Lorenz Flessa, was a teacher). And when Pastor Craemer requested more pastoral help, Löhe responded by sending Eduard Baierlein in June 1847. (Heintzen–1973: 31–33) Pastor Baierlein worked with Craemer until the summer of 1848. Then, Baierlein moved at the request of a band of Indians to make his permanent home in their village, some 60 miles from Frankenmuth. From that point on, this new station, "Bethany," manned by Baierlein and his young wife, replaced Frankenmuth as the center of the colony's missionary work among the American Indians. (Heintzen–1973: 31–33) All told, Pastor Craemer had baptized more than 30 Indian children during the five years that Frankenmuth had functioned as a mission. (cf. Greenholt: 257) The Missouri Synod sought control of the Frankenmuth missions in 1847, and Löhe made the transfer. Unfortunately, "Epidemics of sickness, the migratory habits of the Indians, the tendency of many Indian children to resent discipline and return to their wild haunts, unsatisfactory interpreters, the great distances from the tribes to the school, the interferences of Methodist missionaries, the intrigues of traders and the removal of the Indians by the government caused Frankenmuth to abandon its missionary purpose in favor of the Bethany station." (Greenholt: 257)

When all was said and done, Löhe was responsible for a total of four settlements—Frankenmuth, Frankentrost, Frankenlust, and Frankenhilf. Of these, only Frankenmuth, which was by far the most successful, ever seriously engaged in the Indian mission program Löhe had envisioned.[32]

Now, Löhe very much intended for his colonies to be *German* Lutheran settlements. And it is common to hear some rather harsh criticism of Löhe's insistence on the German language. It may be admitted that he was stereotypically "German" in his stubbornness on this count. "In respect to the distribution of books and funds sent to America Löhe insisted that no English Seminary was to have any claim to them. He warned a *Nothhelfer* in America not to yield a breadth more to the English than was absolutely necessary and useful for the German Lutheran Church. In the *Instructions* to the *Nothhelfer* and in the *Kirchenordnung* there was always a demand for the everlasting use of the German language. He pled as follows with the Germans in America not to exchange their language for the English: 'Your language is next to your Church your greatest jewel. Consider what you forsake if you thoughtlessly discard this noble

[32] For additional information on Löhe's mission to the heathen American Indians, cf. Greenholt, *A Study of Wilhelm Löhe, His Colonies and the Lutheran Indian Missions in the Saginaw Valley of Michigan*; also, Zehnder, *Teach My People the Truth!*; also, Schoenfuhs, "*O Tebeningeion*"—"O Dearest Jesus."

gift of God.'" (Greenholt: 22)

In fairness, however, notwithstanding Löhe's definite bias for the German, he did have good cause for warning against English. The Lutheran synods in America that had switched to English were notoriously unconfessional. (And not surprisingly, since virtually nothing in the way of sound Lutheran literature had yet been translated into English.) Thus, from Löhe's perspective, for the German Lutherans in America to give up their language would be to "abandon their history, the easiest understanding of the Reformation and the true Church of God, their wonderful German Bible, their inspiring songs, their incomparable catechism, their collections of sincere sermons, their books of edification, their liturgies and their domestic literature." (Greenholt: 22) These are surely legitimate concerns. And it is sadly ironic when mission–minded people today, whose battle cry seems to include the almost complete indigenous culturization of liturgy and theology, now also criticize Löhe for his desire to preserve for *German* people the German language and the theological heritage contained by it.

In any case, to facilitate the preservation of the German language and customs, among not only his colonies but all the German Lutheran emigrants, Löhe produced two important German books specifically for use in America. One of these books, Löhe's great *Agende fuer christliche Gemeinden des lutherischen Bekenntnisses* of 1844, has already been discussed. But the other book, his *Haus–, Schul–, und Kirchen–Buch fuer Christen des lutherischen Bekenntnisses* of 1845, is also worthy of note. Fundamentally a catechism, the *Haus–, Schul– und Kirchen–buch* was designed for use in family worship, to supplement the regular church services. Clearly, the point was not merely to give the people something German. Rather, "Löhe realized the shortcomings of most laymen and determined to produce a book which would offer them assistance in the important task of giving spiritual training and nourishment to their families." (Schaaf–1961: 79–81)

> There are many who know the Small Catechism but not its preface which, together with the preface to the Large Catechism, gives an incomparable, simple, truly churchly method of catechetical instruction. There are also many who know

both prefaces without ever having noticed that the catechism was not written only for church and school but also for the home. Home, school, and church together become one Church through the precious catechism... Just as a battle cry should be on the lips of all who belong to an army, so the catechism belongs on all lips as a spiritual battle cry. The father, the children, the servants should use it, pray it, learn it, and treasure it... When the catechism once again becomes a household book we shall learn what sort of strength comes from it for all the Church's activities. (3B: 172–173)

The first section of the *Haus–, Schul– und Kirchen–buch* contains Luther's Small Catechism, accompanied by many Bible passages and explanations by Löhe, designed to support each of the six chief parts. In addition, Löhe includes questions for instruction on special occasions, and a prayer book for children, with detailed instructions and helpful suggestions for teaching the material. A second section, published in 1859, includes "a calendar of the Church Year, a lectionary, a selection of prayers, and a biblical history." (Schaaf–1961: 81–82)[33]

...After Missouri: The Founding of the Iowa Synod:

One of the saddest points in Löhe's life was the ending of his work with the Missouri Synod. After doing so much to give the synod its birth and to support its early growth and development, Löhe found himself caught in the middle of a bitter argument between C. F. W. Walther and Pastor J. A. A. Grabau of the Buffalo Synod. Up for grabs was the doctrine of the Church and Ministry and, as the controversy played itself out, it became obvious that also Walther and Löhe disagreed on the doctrine. As a result, relations between the Neuendettelsau pastor and the Missouri Synod chilled and eventually ended.[34]

---

33 For an English translation of the first section of Löhe's *Haus–, Schul– und Kirchen–buch*, cf. the recently reprinted {Small Catechism...}.
34 For an English translation of Löhe's heartrending farewell letter to the Missouri Synod, cf. MF: 122–125. For additional information on the doctrinal controversy precipitating the break, cf. Stuckwisch, "Whence Comes the Doctrine?"; also, Wohlrabe, *An Historical Analysis of the Doctrine of the Ministry*.

After it first became obvious that Löhe and the Missouri Synod could no longer work together, Pastor Löhe said that he would not interfere with the synod's work but *would* continue his own mission efforts in North America. The final break with Missouri came when he actually tried to do so.

Already in 1850, Löhe had proposed establishing a *Pilgerhaus* in Michigan, to serve as a hospice for German settlers who could there find temporary accommodations before moving on to more permanent settlements. After studying various possibilities, he had chosen Saginaw as the most ideal location. (cf. Heintzen, 1973) By 1852, when the *Pilgerhaus* was actually established, Löhe's primary purpose had changed somewhat. Now he had in mind a hospital for colonists who were ill, and in close connection with it, a teachers' seminary. The students, with their studies, "were to spend their time in caring for the sick, directing the settlers to the colonies, and traveling through the territory in order to serve where needed." Initially, Löhe planned to use the local pastor as the director of both the *Pilgerhaus* and the adjoining seminary. But the project developed so quickly that in 1852 Pastor Georg Grossmann was sent to serve as the seminary's rector. (Schaaf–1961: 93–94) Concerning the new institution, Löhe writes:

> With this moving into the seminary begins a new time. As Pastor Grossmann departed for America we left entirely to him the decision whether or not to join the Missouri Synod. We wished to give the teachers of the seminary full freedom, but not to transfer ownership of the property to the Synod at least until it had achieved a full endowment and a firm foundation and form. We wanted to keep the seminary for ourselves, at least until the aforementioned goal was reached; partly, because we believed that she should be a loyal opposition to the divisive overemphasis on differences, even through a certain amount of independence; partly, because of the experience we had in transferring the Fort Wayne seminary and the Frankenmuth station to the Synod; namely, that through the transfer we died to some extent to our own institutions; so little did our influence then count, that we were assigned simply the support with money and gifts. (Heintzen–1973: 67–68)

Because Grossmann defended Löhe's position in the controversy over Church and Ministry, he declined to join the clergy roster of the Missouri Synod. (cf. Heintzen–1973: 68) And yet, he did become a member of Holy Cross, the Missouri Synod congregation in Saginaw. Grossmann's presence at Holy Cross, coupled with the nearness of Löhe's new seminary, created tensions within the congregation and between Grossmann and the pastor, Ottomar Cloeter (who was himself one of Löhe's missionaries). As the situation came to a head, Wyneken—now the president of the Missouri Synod—strongly "suggested" that the seminary either be transferred to the Missouri Synod, closed down, or moved. Löhe was particularly offended by Wyneken's remark that he and his seminary should: "Go to Iowa; there we don't have any congregations as yet." (Zehnder: 103–105) But by that point, "Pastor Löhe, sick of the controversy with the Missouri Synod, had already decided to move out of Michigan altogether rather than fight the 'new papistical territorialism of the Missouri Synod.' He directed that the seminary be transferred to Iowa before winter." (Heintzen–1973: 69) He writes in a letter to a friend: "The colonists are prospering; the Synod is becoming large; they no longer need us. Where our services are no longer necessary, we must travel on in the work of missions." (Zehnder: 105)

True to his word, Pastor Löhe did move on to continue the work of missions in North America. In October 1853, those who remained loyal to their Neuendettelsau father in Christ crossed the Mississippi River at Dubuque, Iowa, and immediately re-opened the teachers' seminary under Grossmann's direction. The group included two pastors—Grossmann and Deindoerfer, the former pastor of Löhe's Frankenhilf colony—two students, and 18 colonists. Pastor Deindoerfer and those colonists who were farmers purchased land 60 miles farther west and there established the St. Sebald settlement (named for the first missionary to bring the Gospel to their native home of Nuremberg, Bavaria). These two congregations, in Dubuque and St. Sebald, formed the Iowa Synod in 1854 and from such small beginnings, the new synod grew quickly. "Löhe continued to send trained pastors as well as money for the school, which soon turned to preparing men for the clergy as well as parochial school teachers. Within 5 years the synod numbered 28 congregations and 25 pastors; by 1864 it counted more than 50 congregations in 7 states, with 41 clergy." By the end of 1857, after the seminary had moved from Dubuque to St. Sebald and had taken the name of *Wartburg*, the school had 16 students. The full course of study included four years of "pre–seminary" education and three years of theological study. And as evidence of Löhe's continued desire to evangelize the American Indians, several of the first students to graduate from Wartburg Seminary volunteered for work among the Indians to the west. One of these graduates, Pastor Moritz Braeuninger, had been trained as a carpenter in Saxony but was recruited by Löhe to go to America, complete theological studies, and become a pastor of the Iowa Synod. He served on at least two missionary outings to the Crows in Montana and Wyoming. On the second of these outings, he was martyred for his efforts to share the Gospel with the American Indians. (Schmutterer: 118–127)

The Neuendettelsau Society for Inner Missions:

By the time the Iowa Synod was formed in 1854, Löhe's direct, personal involvement in the mission to America had become far less significant—not that his impact and influence had disappeared, but that direction of the work had by then been given primarily to others. It is important to remember that, all the while he was directing activities in America, Löhe was also the pastor of a thriving congregation. By 1849, his American projects had begun to overwhelm a disproportionate amount of his time. So in September of that year, Löhe and 33 of his friends established a missionary society, the "*Gesellschaft fuer innere Mission nach dem Sinne der lutherischen Kirche*." (cf. Schaaf–1961: 91–92)

> "Inner mission," as Löhe understood the term, was not limited to a particular place and could not be separated from "foreign mission." "Inner" in the name of the missionary society indicated that it was an organization for the Lutheran Church. It carried out the work of sending preachers and teachers to America and later to other lands, distributing books and tracts, advising and assisting colonists, and engaging in charitable work in Germany. (3B: 24n78)

Though Löhe served as chairman of the missionary society from its beginning until 1862, one of the chief results of its formation was that Löhe relinquished much of his personal responsibility for the activities in America. The work that he had started almost single-handedly could now be handled directly by a large group of dedicated people. In fact, by the time Löhe retired as chairman of the *Gesellschaft*, in 1862, the number of members had increased to 515 men and women. Pastor Löhe was thus free to direct his personal attention to local activities. (cf. Schaaf–1961: 93)

LÖHE'S LOCAL MISSION— THE DEACONESS MOTHERHOUSE:

Of the local activities to which Pastor Wilhelm Löhe directed his attention, the most outstanding is the Deaconess Motherhouse of Neuendettelsau. In 1853, he proposed a project for the training of women to care for the sick. He envisioned establishing institutions, centered around hospitals, in which the daughters of middle–class families could be trained as nurses and receive a general education. He hoped that graduates might serve not only as nurses in hospitals, but also individually in their own homes and congregations. (cf. Ottersberg: 182) Löhe writes of three reasons for his consideration of such a female diaconate:

> (1.) We find everywhere some women who care for the ill and miserable more than others do, because they are enticed to do that work through a special gift within them. They are following a natural urge. What they need is the training of this gift. Many of these women would be Biblical deaconesses if one were interested enough to give them the necessary training...
> (2.) Now, since there are many young gifted women in this middle class in the flat (farming) country, they become spiritually and mentally crippled because of lack of training, and frequently use their gifts in a baneful way for the ruination of the real country people. But, if an interest were taken in them they would become very able and influential bearers and representatives of godly and useful thoughts. There would be

no better way of showing an interest in them than to prepare an opportunity for the training of their gifts in behalf of suffering humanity. They would be led as a result into a useful life, would have an occupation, and indeed would find a holy and blessed position in the Church, and would become the most suitable means of Christian education for the country folk. In witnessing their service to the ill and at death–beds, many would learn much, and to be sure the service of nursing. Moreover, they would be blessed and be a blessing—to the ill directly, and indirectly to the entire female population... (3.) Doubtless, many Christian families in the country would be glad to give their daughters an opportunity to spend a short period of time in an institution so agreeably fitted to the nature of women, where they could receive definite guidance for their own benefit, and where they could learn and acquire experience along so many lines which would be of greatest value for their daily home–life!" (Schober: 97)

Löhe's idea took concrete shape in 1854, when the Deaconess Motherhouse opened in Neuendettelsau (cf. Ottersberg: 183). He writes of his intentions:

We wanted to train our own people for our own needs, and to that end did not have it in mind to settle in larger cities, but on the contrary, we searched for quiet places where we could reach the daughters of the country and train them for the relief of our distress. Not permanently, but just for the present we planned to settle in Neuendettelsau and try to make a beginning with a small institution for fallen women and retarded children, which was to become beneficial to our own people in a short period of time. (Schober: 98)

Initially, the idea had been to prompt the organization of similar societies throughout Bavaria. But when those hopes failed, Löhe concentrated his efforts entirely on the Neuendettelsau Motherhouse. It began with a hospital, and with various schools for both women and girls. Even young girls were admitted to be trained in preparation for teaching. Soon this developed into three distinct schools: an elementary school, a preparatory school, and the deaconess school itself. "Löhe himself took charge of instruction as well as of general management, while the deaconesses...took charge of the details of administration. A physician gave medical instruction." (Ottersberg: 182–183)

The Deaconess Motherhouse grew slowly but steadily over the years. And it was gradually surrounded by a whole complex of institutions. "Houses were established for the education of women, for the care of the ill and sickly, for work with degraded persons, for paramentics, the preparation of [Communion] wafers, and the domestic Economy with all its varied work." (Schober: 104) "The complex of charitable... institutions and their work developed by [Löhe] in Neuendettelsau became world renowned, and earned the title of 'university of mercy.' A mere listing of the institutions is impressive. Among them were a deaconess home (1854), a house of rescue (1862), house for mentally ill (1864), home for fallen girls (1865), hospital for men (1867), hospital for women (1869)." (Heintzen–1964: 31–32) In addition, a large assembly hall was erected for the service of the institution's congregation; a predecessor of the present institution–church of St. Laurentius. (cf. Schober: 104) What is more, "deaconesses trained in Neuendettelsau have served throughout Germany and in many parts of the world." (3B: 26) Rightly does Löhe record high praises for these women:

> If I were an artist... I would paint the deaconess as she should be in her various life situations and labors. There would be a whole row of pictures. I would paint the maiden in the stable and at the Altar; in the laundry and how she attires the naked in clean linen of compassion; in the kitchen and in the hospital ward; in the field and at the Sanctus in the choir, and when she sings the Nunc Dimittis for the communicants. I would paint every deaconess calling, but in all of them a maiden, not always with a veil, but always a person... and why? Because a deaconess should know how to and be willing to perform the most lowly and the noblest kind of women's work; she should not be ashamed to do the humblest and not ruin the most sublime. The feet in the dust of humble work, the hands at the harp, the head in the sunlight of devotion and knowl-

edge of Jesus—thus I would paint her on the frontispiece of the entire collection of pictures. Underneath I would write: She is capable of doing everything: Work, play, sing praises. (Schober: 105–106)[35]

LÖHE'S FINAL DAYS AND DEATH:

Rightly would high praises be sung of Pastor Wilhelm Löhe himself, for his powerful, life-long witness to his faith and to the Gospel of his dear Lord Jesus Christ. His tireless efforts on behalf of the Church he loved so dearly continued nigh unto his death on January 2, 1872. Even during the last half year of his life, he preached off and on. "But shortly before Christmas 1871 he... had an attack of exhaustion. On the day before Christmas he received Holy Communion and began to feel stronger. But his thoughts were directed toward the end. New Year's Day, sitting in the corner of his couch, he received congratulations on the part of many and the wish that he be able to walk again and enjoy the fresh air. 'Then it would surely be better if I could preach again,' was his significant answer." That very afternoon he suffered a stroke from which he never regained consciousness, and after "a prolonged death struggle supported by intercessory prayer," he was finally called to his heavenly home at the age of 63 years. (Schober: 108)

Appropriately, for Löhe's burial on January 5, 1872 (for which he had requested that there be no sermon given) the following words of Scripture were read: *Many who lie asleep under the earth will wake up; some to eternal life, others to eternal scandal and shame. The teachers however will shine like the splendor of Heaven and those who lead many to righteousness as the stars forever!* (cf. Schober: 108–109)

THE CONTINUING FRUITS OF LÖHE'S EFFORTS:

Behind him, Wilhelm Löhe left a living testimony to his life

---

[35] For additional information on the Deaconess Motherhouse, cf. Suelflow, "Centennial of the Neuendettelsau Deaconess Institute."

of service. In addition to all that he had accomplished for the sake of the Gospel during his lifetime, his Neuendettelsau institutions continued to serve the cause of missions around the world even after his death. In 1878, "the first two mission candidates from Neuendettelsau went to Australia, and another eight years later Johannes Flierl from Neuendettelsau arrived as the first missionary in New Guinea for the Kaiser–Wilhelmland." (Schober: 93)[36]

> We find people from Neuendettelsau—apart from the distress areas in Germany—in Aden, France, Holland, Austria, Poland, Slovakia, Russia, Scotland, and in East Africa. But above all in the laboring areas of North America, Australia, New Guinea, and Brazil. Even now [in 1959] the recruits for the ministry in Brazil [are] in large measure covered by candidates from the seminary in Neuendettelsau. They also go to Columbia and after the First World War to Palestine and the Ukraine. (Schober: 94)

Such is the living legacy of a great man of God, *Johannes Konrad Wilhelm Löhe.*

> AND I HEARD A VOICE FROM HEAVEN, SAYING, "WRITE, 'BLESSED ARE THE DEAD WHO DIE IN THE LORD FROM NOW ON!'" "YES," SAYS THE SPIRIT, "THAT THEY MAY REST FROM THEIR LABORS, FOR THEIR DEEDS FOLLOW WITH THEM." (REVELATION 14:13)

---

36 [36] For additional information, cf. e.g. Löhe (Max), "The Wilhelm Löhe—Neuendettelsau Influence in the Lutheran Church of Australia."

A FINAL WORD FROM WILHELM LÖHE: We know that all other confessions which preach to the heathen bring them the possibility of salvation. Therefore, we are pleased with the missions of all confessions, even though we regret their doctrinal deficiencies and the errors they practice. We pray for all missions, not that their partisan objectives may be achieved but that the truths they proclaim may be blessed with the salvation of the heathen. With goodwill and inner longing we follow the results of all missions and rejoice over everything good the others accomplish through the doctrines which they have taken from us.

But that is not all.

We pray the Lord to forgive our sin for having done too little for the salvation of the heathen. We know that this must be changed. After having long enough through our treasures enabled others to preach their less pure doctrines, we ourselves are finally going out to preach the pure Word of life to all people. Although we are a small flock, the Lord will give us a host of evangelists who will go out into the highways and byways of the heathen and testify to them of the universal grace of God in Christ Jesus. As the Lord increases our numbers in the old lands of Christen-

dom, He will strengthen us, and the fervor of our united love will prove itself stronger and more powerful among the heathen. We pray the Lord to fill our hands for the salvation of the heathen, and He will do it!
(Three Books About the Church)

APPENDIX: LÖHE'S AMERICAN CONTEMPORARIES, WALTHER AND GRABAU

Despite their disagreements over the doctrine of the Church and Ministry, Löhe had much in common with Pastors C. F. Walther and J. A. A. Grabau.[37] Chiefly, they were united in a love for, and adherence to, their confessional Lutheran heritage, even when they differed in their interpretation of that heritage. Among other aspects of this shared confessional Lutheranism, Löhe's contemporaries in America also maintained a similar liturgical theology in many respects. Each of the three men produced an agenda for use among the German Lutherans of America, and each man drew upon the historic Lutheran orders to formulate his own order. An extensive treatment of the similarites and differences between Löhe, Walther, and Grabau would go far beyond the scope of this present work. Nevertheless, some brief observations will be made.[38]

Pastor C. F. W. Walther:

Walther knew from personal experience the importance of orthodox liturgical forms. In his first parish, in Braensdorf, Saxony, he had been penalized for using the old Lutheran form of the general absolution, which was not included in the official agenda. In general, "Pastors and congregations were subjected to a number of liturgical abuses at this time." (Marzolf: 85)[39] "Walther realized the confes-

37 For information on the controversy over Church and Ministry, cf. the author's "Whence Comes the Doctrine," *Reflections* (student journal of Concordia Theological Seminary, Fort Wayne, IN), vol. 7, no. 1 (Fall 1991), pp. 16–30.
38 The information on Walther and Grabau presented herein is drawn almost exclusively from Marzolf's "C. F. W. Walther: The Musician and Liturgiologist" and the Brenners' "J. A. A. Grabau: The Restoration of Orthodox Worship." Precious little is available in English on the liturgical theology of these two important figures, especially in the case of Pastor Grabau. To the victor go the spoils, as they say, and Grabau lost. Thus, we here make do with what is available. References to the above sources are cited only in the case of direct quotations.
39 Marzolf provides some specific examples of the abuses:
> Prayers provided by the official agencies for use on special occasions were clearly unscriptural. A rationalistic hymnal had replaced and paraphrased the old Lutheran hymns with new versions that perverted the

sional implications of liturgical practice. Liturgical forms were not mere 'window dressing' for the sermon in Walther's liturgy. In fact, the sermon is seen to be a part of the liturgical flow that blossoms forth from the Holy Gospel and the Creed; a part that finally fills the House of the Lord with sweet aroma of the prayers of the faithful. " (Marzolf: 92)

In the early days of the Missouri Synod, a number of different liturgical books were being used among its congregations: various hymnals and agendas that had come with the Germans into America. Among these books—in addition to Löhe's *Agende*—were various editions of the Saxon agendas dating from the 17th century. Such a proliferation of resources was confusing, and so, in order to promote unity, Walther took in hand the task of preparing a new Missouri Synod hymnal and a new agenda.[40]

---

doctrine and poetry of the originals. The chorale melodies that were the heritage of the confessional Lutheran church were cast aside, rhythmically altered, and harmonically mutilated so as to render them lifeless and weak...

The church agenda was full of doctrinal error. Of the five baptismal forms in the book only one was suitable for use by the Christian pastor. The already weak forms were made even weaker by pastors who deleted and altered the structures of the service in an extemporaneous manner. Liturgical license was a theme of the day, with the result that the teachings of Scripture, as they had been clearly proclaimed in the creeds and prayers of the Church, were lost. (Marzolf: 85)

40 The desire for liturgical unity and "the greatest possible uniformity in ceremonies" is evident in several articles of the First Synodical Constitution of the Missouri Synod. A lengthy explanation of this desire is also provided:

Synod holds in accordance with the 7th article of the Augsburg Confession that uniformity in ceremonies is not essential; yet on the other hand Synod deems such a uniformity wholesome and useful, namely for the following reasons:

(a.) because a total difference in outward ceremonies would cause those who are weak in the unity of doctrine to stumble;

(b.) because in dropping heretofore preserved usages the Church is to avoid the appearance of and desire for innovations;

Furthermore Synod deems it necessary for the purification of the Lutheran Church in America, that the emptiness and the poverty in the externals of the service be opposed, which, having been introduced here by the false spirit of the Reformed, is now rampant.

Much after the style of Löhe's prayer books, Walther's hymnal (first published in 1847) clearly followed the Church Year in its arrangement of the hymns. "It is evident that the editor views the Church Year as one of the effective tools for teaching doctrines of Lutheranism, for by following the Church Year all the teachings of Scripture are proclaimed." (Marzolf: 87)

The hymns themselves reflect a conscious effort to retain the classical Lutheran faith in its piety as well as its doctrine. The predominance of hymns are chosen from the 16th– and 17th–century hymnists, in both their texts and chorale melodies. With respect to his judgment of the melodies preserved in the hymnal, it is important to note that, unlike Löhe, Walther did have talent for, and a strong background in, music. "He enjoyed music, but more importantly he *knew* music. He had studied it, and he was able to approach performance as a disciplined amateur." (Marzolf: 84) The most important criteria for choosing the hymns are explained by Walther (presumably) in an an unsigned article of *Der Lutheraner*:

> In the selection of the adopted hymns the chief consideration was that they be pure in doctrine; that they have found almost universal acceptance with the orthodox German Lutheran Church and have thus received the almost unanimous testimony that they had come forth from the true spirit [of Lutheranism]; that they express not so much the changing circumstances of individual persons but rather contain the language of the whole Church, because the book is to be used primarily in public worship; and finally that they, though bearing the imprint of Christian simplicity, be not merely rhymed prose but the creations of a truly Christian poetry...
>
> [The editors] selected only those hymns which they recognized as particularly worthy of transmission from children to children's children and of preservation as a treasure, as an inalienable possession of the German–speaking Church... We are also of the opinion that we have great cause to

---

All pastors and congregations that wish to be recognized as orthodox by Synod are prohibited from adopting or retaining any ceremony which might weaken the confession of the truth or condone or strengthen a heresy, especially if heretics insist upon the continuation or the abolishing of such ceremonies. (Polack: 11–12)

be concerned about the proper preservation of the wonderful, rich treasury of our church melodies. (MF: 182–183)

In similar fashion, in his *Agenda* of 1856, Walther demonstrates "his appreciation and understanding of the old liturgical forms." (Marzolf: 92) As with Löhe, Walther is not out to "fix" what is not broken; instead, he "joyfully built on the old foundation when he constructed the Agenda." (Marzolf: 90) Sadly, because it was produced so soon after the break between the Missouri Synod and Löhe (1854), Walther's *Agenda* seems to be drawn far more heavily from the older Saxon agendas than from Löhe's *magnum opus*. Nevertheless, while Walther's liturgy is simpler than Löhe's, "it [is] no less churchly." (Marzolf: 89)

Precisely because Walther and many of his fellow Saxons did have a high regard for the churchly, liturgical traditions of the Lutheran Church, they, too, were accused of "Romanizing." In response to a complaint specifically about the practice of chanting, Walther (presumably) published another unsigned article in *Der Lutheraner*. His argumentation is as brilliant as it is pointed, and it certainly echoes the sentiments of Löhe no less than Walther's own.

> Wherever the Divine Service once again follows the old Evangelical Lutheran agendas or church books it seems that many raise a great cry that it is "Roman Catholic" when the pastor sings "The Lord be with you" and the congregation responds by singing "And with thy spirit"; or if the pastor sings the collect and the blessing and the people respond with a sung "Amen." Even the simplest Christian can respond to this outcry, "Prove to me that this chanting is contrary to the Word of God, then I, too, will call it 'Roman Catholic' and have nothing more to do with it. However, you cannot prove this to me. If you insist upon calling every element in the Divine Service 'Roman' that has been used by the Roman Catholic Church, it must follow that the reading of the Epistle and Gospel is also 'Romish'; indeed, it is mischief to sing or preach in church, for the Roman church has also done this."...
> Those who cry out should remember that the Roman Catholic Church possesses every beautiful song of the old orthodox

Church; the chants and antiphons and responses were brought into the Church long before the false teaching of Rome crept in... For more than 1700 years orthodox Christian have joyfully participated in the Divine Service; should we today carry on that such joyful participation is "Roman Catholic"? God prevent it.

Therefore, as we continue to hold and restore our wonderful Divine Services in places where they have been forgotten, let us boldly confess that our worship forms do not unite us with the modern sects or the church of Rome, rather they join us to the one, holy Christian Church that is as old as the world and is built on the foundation of the apostles and prophets. (Marzolf: 89–90)

Finally, it should be noted that Walther was the professor in charge of "Liturgics with exercises in singing" at the St. Louis Seminary, at least in 1860. (MF: 218) No doubt his background in music and his experience with the new hymnal and agenda made Walther the obvious choice for this task.

Pastor J. A. A. Grabau:

While Löhe and Walther experienced opposition and endured criticism in reaction to their efforts to recapture and retain a traditional Lutheran cultus, Johannes Grabau was made most painfully aware of the difficulties involved in this task. He emigrated from Germany to America specifically to escape the legally mandated use of the Prussian Union Agenda.[41] He "had been deposed and jailed by the civil authorities in Germany for his insistent adherence to old Lutheran practice." (Brenner: 95) Pastor L. F. E. Krause, another Prussian emigrate associated with Grabau, provides a telling description of the situation as they saw it:

When the devil saw that his work of confusion was

---

[41] "The Prussian king [Friedrich Wilhelm III] knew that the cause of the Union would be furthered by the adoption of a common Agenda. An administrative order on 30 April 1830 authorized the use of the power of the state to overcome resistance to the Union" (MF: 60).

started, then he took his main step and brought about the union on June 25 in the year of the Lord 1830. For this purpose he made use of the secular power of the king of Prussia, Friedrich Wilhelm III. This Reformed potentate was brought to that point by his two court preachers Eylert and Neander, who had for a long time already been discussing such a false union between Reformed and Lutherans, that he gave out a mandate under his name in 1830 that every pastor should without hesitation accept the United—the so-called Evangelical State Church—church book under threat of removal from office.

This church book of the new state church (united sect) is a disorderly mess. The liturgy is taken from the prayer book of the English Reformed Episcopal Church, the formulas and prayers for Baptism and the Lord's Supper are taken from several German Reformed agendas, as also the collects, and the crown of this monstrosity is the Egyptian funeral ceremony. Here and there the name of the Triune God is interpolated to attract those who still believe that; for most of the pastors were Socinians. The Reformed, whose doctrine is Socinian through and through, whether coarse or fine, were very willing to accept this agenda. And why shouldn't they? For it was their doctrine which was in the agenda. (MF: 126)

Coming from this background, it is not surprising that Pastor Grabau rather quickly prepared an agenda for use among his Lutheran congregations in America. Nor is it surprising that Grabau's agenda emphasized "a restored Lutheran liturgy" and provided for "a heightened appreciation and use of the means of grace, and of the divine service." (Brenner: 94) These characteristics of his agenda may be seen not only as a positive confession of the Lutheran faith, but also as a reaction and protest against the Reformed denigrations of the liturgy and Sacraments in Grabau's Prussian homeland. "Grabau was not trying to be creative, to make something altogether new and unknown, or something totally American." (Brenner: 95) Far from it. His intention was to restore what had already been lost or was in danger of being lost from the historic Lutheran liturgy.[42]

In the introductory remarks of his *Hirtenbrief*, Grabau comments on the proper use of religious freedom which the Lutheran Church enjoys in America. He gives thanks to God for this gift of freedom, but he also cautions the Church in her use of it. In this context, he warns against the "abuse of church freedom against any article of the Faith or against *any part of the worship service (Gottesdienst)*," which "would keep us from the purpose of our emigration from the land of church oppression." (Grabau: 1; emphasis added) It would hardly do for the Prussian Lutherans, having fled the Union Agenda, to abuse their newfound freedom by adopting corrupt liturgical practices.

Grabau's *Hirtenbrief*—written primarily to address the importance of a regular call (*rite vocatus*)—also discusses the use of certain "customs of the Church, for example candles and a crucifix on the altar, the sign of the cross, chanting the collects and blessings as well as the responses." (Grabau: 6) One may assume that Grabau, too, had been accused of "Romanizing" tendencies in his liturgical practices. In response, he explains the meaning and purpose of such customs in a thoroughly evangelical and pastoral manner. He writes in conclusion:

> Who fears such [customs]? Or who would disdain such? How should such standing reminders [of Jesus Christ] not do our frivolous and forgetful hearts good? Therefore, the Church does right when she keeps such things, even when she knows that such ceremonies *of themselves* neither help nor hurt our salvation, for *candles and the cross of themselves* cannot either help nor hurt, *but the right use of such ceremonies*, which are not against God's Word, can be useful for the soul. (Grabau: 6)

---

42 Accordingly, "Not only did Grabau represent and preserve the forms of Luther's Formula of the Mass, intended by Luther for the principal, city churches of his day; Grabau also incorporated options which allowed congregations, according to the means at their disposal, to follow Luther's German Mass designed for the smaller, less formal parish churches" (Brenner: 95–96). By way of another example, though Grabau does include a general confession in his principal Sunday Service, he "favors and promotes the old lutheran custom of private confession before communion" (Brenner: 97).

BIBLIOGRAPHY:

Brenner, Karl and Marie. "J. A. A. Grabau: The Restoration of Orthodox Worship." In *Confessional Lutheran Migrations to America: 150th Anniversary.* [East Amherst, NY]: Eastern District, LC—MS, 1988.

Conser, Walter H., Jr. *Church and Confession: Conservative Theologians in Germany, England, and America 1815–1866.* Macon, GA: Mercer University Press, 1984.

──────. "A Conservative Critique of Church and State: The Case of the Tractarians and Neo–Lutherans." *Journal of Church and State*, vol. 25, no. 2 (Spring 1983), pp. 323–341.

Grabau, J. A. A. Pastoral Letter [1 December 1840]. Unpublished translation by Brian Heidt. Fort Wayne, IN: 199–.

Greenholt, Homer Reginald. *A Study of Wilhelm Loehe, His Colonies and the Lutheran Indian Missions in the Saginaw Valley of Michigan.* An unpublished dissertation submitted to the faculty of the University of Chicago Divinity School, in candidacy for the degree of Doctor of Philosophy. Chicago, IL: June 1937.

Heintzen, Erich Hugo. *Wilhelm Loehe and the Missouri Synod, 1841–1853.* An unpublished thesis submitted in partial fulfillment of the requirements for the degree of Doctor of Philosophy in History, in the Graduate College of the University of Illinois. Urbana, IL: 1964.

──────. *Love Leaves Home: Wilhelm Loehe and the Missouri Synod.* Condensed by Frank Starr. St. Louis, MO: Concordia Publishing House, 1973.

Kantzenbach, F. W. "Wilhelm Loehe—100 Years Later." Translated by Rev. Wilhelm Torgerson. *The Springfielder*, vol. 35, no. 3 (December 1971), pp. 191–196.

Korby, Kenneth Frederick. *The Theology of Pastoral Care in Wilhelm Loehe With Special Attention to the Function of the Liturgy and the Laity.* A Th.D. dissertation, Concordia Seminary in Exile in cooperation with Lutheran School of Theology, 1976.

Ann Arbor, MI: University Microfilms International, 1981.
Lockwood, Gregory. *The Peace of the Kingdom: A Study of the Concept of "Peace" in the New Testament and Lutheran Missiology*. A Dissertation presented to the faculty of Concordia Seminary, St. Louis, Department of Exegetical Theology, in partial fulfillment of the requirements for the degree of Doctor of Theology. St. Louis, MO: November 1983. Fort Wayne, IN: Concordia Theological Seminary Press.
Loehe, Max. "The Wilhelm Loehe—Neuendettelsau Influence in the Lutheran Church of Australia." *The Springfielder*, vol. 35, no. 3 (December 1971), pp. 183–190.
Löhe, Wilhelm. *Liturgy for Christian Congregations of the Lutheran Faith*, Third Edition. Edited by J. Deinzer. Translated by F. C. Longaker, with introduction by Edward T. Horn. Newport, KY: 1902. Reprinted by Repristination Press, Fort Wayne, IN: 1993.

_____. *Loehe on Prayer*. Unpublished translations of various writings of Wilhelm Löhe on corporate and individual prayer. Translated by Dennis W. Marzolf. Fort Wayne, IN: 198–.

_____. *Seed–Grains of Prayer: A Manual for Evangelical Christians*. Translation from the original German 36th Edition. Translated by H. A. Weller, with introduction by Henry Eyster Jacobs. Columbus, OH: The Wartburg Press, 1912.

_____. *Questions and Answers to the Six Parts of the Small Catechism of Dr. Martin Luther. Translation from the Fourth Edition of the House– School– and Church–Book for Christians of the Lutheran Faith*. Translated by Edward T. Horn. Columbia, SC: W. J. Duffie, 1893. Reprinted by Repristination Press, Fort Wayne, IN: 1993.

_____. Three Books About the Church. Translated and edited, with introduction by James L. Schaaf. Reprinted by permission of Augsburg Fortress Press. Fort Wayne, IN: Concordia Theological Seminary Press, 1989.
Lueker, Erwin L., Editor. *Lutheran Cyclopedia: A Concise In–Home Reference for the Christian Family*. Revised Edition. St. Louis, MO: Concordia Publishing House, 1975.
Marzolf, Dennis W. "C. F. W. Walther: The Musician and Liturgiolo-

gist." In *C. F. W. Walther: The American Luther*. Essays in Commemoration of the 100th Anniversary of Carl Walther's Death. Mankato, MN: Walther Press, 1987.

Meyer, Carl S., editor. *Moving Frontiers: Readings in the History of the Lutheran Church—Missouri Synod*. St. Louis, MO: Concordia Publishing House, 1964.

⎯⎯⎯. "Johann Konrad Wilhelm Loehe—In Memoriam." *Concordia Theological Monthly*, vol. 43, no. 7 (July–August 1972), pp. 442–445.

Nichol, Todd. "Wilhelm Loehe, the Iowa Synod and the Ordained Ministry." *Lutheran Quarterly*, vol. 4, no. 1 (Spring 1990), pp. 11–29.

Ottersberg, Gerhard. "Wilhelm Loehe." *The Lutheran Quarterly*, vol. 4, no. 2 (May 1952), pp. 170–190.

Polack, W. G., editor. "Our First Synodical Constitution." *Concordia Historical Institute Quarterly*, vol. 16, no. 1 (April 1943), pp. 1–18.

Sasse, Herman. "Walther and Loehe: On The Church." Translated and prepared by John Sippola and John Drickamer. *The Springfielder*, vol. 35, no. 3 (December 1971), pp. 176–182.

Schaaf, James Lewis. *Wilhelm Loehe's Relation to the American Church: A Study in the History of Lutheran Mission*. An unpublished Inaugural–Dissertation, zur Erlangung der Wuerde eines Doktors der Evangelisch–Theologischen Fakultaet der Ruprecht–Karl–Universitaet zu Heidelberg. 1961.

⎯⎯⎯. "Wilhelm Loehe and the Missouri Synod." *Concordia Historical Institute Quarterly*, vol. 45, no. 2 (May 1972), pp. 53–67.

⎯⎯⎯. "The Genesis of a Worldwide Mission Thrust." *Lutheran Theological Journal*, vol. 22, no. 3 (December 1988), pp. 129–134.

Schattauer, Thomas H. "Sunday Worship at Neuendettelsau Under Wilhelm Loehe." *Worship*, vol. 59, no. 4 (July 1985), pp. 370–384.

⎯⎯⎯. *Announcement, Confession, and Lord's Supper in the Pastoral–Liturgical Work of Wilhelm Löhe: A Study of Worship and Church Life in the Lutheran Parish at Neuendettelsau*,

Bavaria, 1837–1872. An unpublished dissertation submitted to the Graduate School of the University of Notre Dame, in partial fulfillment of the requirements for the degree of Doctor of Philosophy. Notre Dame, IN: June 1990.

Schmutterer, Gerhard M., and Charles P. Lutz. "Mission Martyr on the Wester Frontier: Can Cross–Cultural Mission Be Achieved?" In *Church Roots: Stories of Nine Immigrant Groups That Became The American Lutheran Church.* Edited by Charles P. Lutz. Minneapolis, MN: Augsburg Publishing House, 1985.

Schober, Theodor. *Wilhelm Loehe: Witness of the Living Lutheran Church.* Translated by Sister Bertha Mueller from Wilhelm Löhe: Ein zeuge lebendiger lutherischer Kirche. Giessen, Germany: Brunnen–Verlag, 1959.

Schoenfuhs, Walter P. "O Tebeningeion"—"O Dearest Jesus." *Concordia Historical Institute Quarterly,* vol. 37, no. 3 (October 1964), pp. 95–114.

Suelflow, Aug. R. "Centennial of the Neuendettelsau Deaconess Institute, 1854–1954." *Concordia Theological Monthly,* vol. 25, no. 9 (September 1954), pp. 672–674.

Weis, James. *The Place of the Lutheran Confessions in Lutheranism Past and Present: An Historical Survey.* An unpublished faculty study paper, Concordia Theological Seminary. Springfield, IL: October 1968.

Wittenberg, Martin. "Wilhelm Loehe and Confession: A Contribution to the History of Seelsorge and the Office of the Ministry within Modern Lutheranism." Translated by Gerald S. Krispin. In *And Every Tongue Confess: Essays in Honor of Norman Nagel on the Occasion of His Sixty–Fifth Birthday.* Edited by Gerald S. Krispin and Jon D. Vieker. Copyright by The Nagel Festschrift Committee, 1990. Chelsea, MI: BookCrafters.

Wohlrabe, John C., Jr. *An Historical Analysis of the Doctrine of the Ministry in the Lutheran Church—Missouri Synod Until 1962.* An unpublished dissertation presented to the faculty of Concordia Seminary, St. Louis, Department of Historical Theology, in partial fulfillment of the requirements for the degree of Doctor of Theology. St. Louis, MO: May 1987.

Wyneken, F. C. D. *The Distress of the German Lutherans in North America*. Translated by S. Edgar Schmidt. Edited by R. F. Rehmer. Printed by permission of Clifton H. Johnson, American Home Missionary Society Archives, Amistad Research Center, New Orleans, Louisiana. Fort Wayne, IN: Concordia Theological Seminary Press, 1986.

Zehnder, Herman F. *"Teach My People the Truth!": The Story of Frankenmuth, Michigan*. Frankenmuth, MI: Published by author, 1970.

+ Soli Deo Gloria — Sola Mea Culpa +

CPSIA information can be obtained at www.ICGtesting.com
Printed in the USA
LVOW122100100113

315227LV00019BA/1376/P